(un)Natural Mom

"Our culture puts so much pressure on moms to be perfect. Hettie Brittz reminds us that the 'supermom' is a myth and encourages mothers to embrace their unique temperaments and gifts as they raise their kids."

Jim Daly, president of Focus on the Family

"Hettie offers hope to a broken world where today's moms and dads often feel guilty about their own imperfect parenting."

Jonathan McKee, author of *52 Ways to Connect with Your Smartphone Obsessed Kid*

(un)Natural Mom

(un)Natural Mom

Why *You* Are the Perfect Mom for Your Kids

Hettie Brittz

David C Cook

transforming lives together

(UN)NATURAL MOM
Published by David C Cook
4050 Lee Vance View
Colorado Springs, CO 80918 U.S.A.

David C Cook U.K., Kingsway Communications
Eastbourne, East Sussex BN23 6NT, England

The graphic circle C logo is a registered trademark of David C Cook.

The website addresses recommended throughout this book are offered as a
resource to you. These websites are not intended in any way to be or imply an
endorsement on the part of David C Cook, nor do we vouch for their content.

Details in some stories have been changed to protect
the identities of the persons involved.

Unless otherwise noted, all Scripture quotations are taken from THE MESSAGE.
Copyright © by Eugene H. Peterson 1993, 2002. Used by permission of NavPress.
All rights reserved. Represented by Tyndale House Publishers, Inc. Scripture
quotations marked NIV are taken from the Holy Bible, NEW INTERNATIONAL
VERSION®, NIV®. Copyright © 1973, 2011 by Biblica, Inc.® Used by permission.
All rights reserved worldwide. NEW INTERNATIONAL VERSION® and
NIV® are registered trademarks of Biblica, Inc. Use of either trademark for the
offering of goods or services requires the prior written consent of Biblica, Inc.

LCCN 2016933708
ISBN 978-1-4347-1028-4
eISBN 978-1-4347-1065-9

The Team: Kyle Duncan, Erin Healy, Nick Lee, Cara Iverson, Susan Murdock
Cover Design: Amy Konyndyk
Cover Photo: Getty Images/Jamie Grill

Printed in the United States of America
First Edition 2016

1 2 3 4 5 6 7 8 9 10

052616

To all the moms, stepmoms, and grandmas who
get "the look" more often than they give it

*There's no way to be a perfect mother and a
million ways to be a good one.*

Jill Churchill, author

Contents

Preface

In *(un)Natural Mom*, you'll find out how to determine your parenting temperament so you can fully embrace God's design for you as a mom. The Tall Trees Parenting Profile (T^2P^2) is a free and private online tool created just for this purpose.

We encourage you to take the T^2P^2 now by creating an account at www.talltreestraining.com, where you can log in and follow the (un)Natural Mom links. Your profile test will identify your unique tree type and show you the result of your three-dimensional mothering style (your Nurture Profile, Discipline Profile, and Mentor Profile). The T^2P^2 is also suited to dads, grandparents, and caregivers.

An optional, more detailed personal report that goes beyond the contents of this book is available for purchase. The report will explore each one of your parenting-style components in greater detail. It also contains a complete growth plan with life-coaching questions that will help you Embrace, Explore, Explain, and Expand your mothering characteristics. If you wish to buy this piece, you can activate a discount by answering a question about this book, located on the website.

Introduction

All of us moms know those moments when shame and dread wash over us because we have fallen short of the ideal of the Natural Mother. Our child is the only one to show up after summer break without the complete set of school supplies. We lost the list, started too late, or thought that the list was a mere suggestion when in fact it was the eleventh commandment. We wonder if we'll ever get our mothering act together before we cause permanent damage. We already feed our children the occasional plate of junk food, sometimes put them to bed without a Bible story, and often scream when we should say, "Sweetie, let's calm down"—to ourselves first, then to our children, unless they have already run off to save themselves.

How many failures are we allowed before resigning ourselves to the title of (un)Natural Mom? Many parenting books don't allow us many. They tell us the five characteristics every good mom should have and the seven steps we must take to be true Christian mothers. We cringe as we add up our scores. Books abound about "natural" ways to do everything from giving birth to letting go, and every one of these books sticks a finger right in our eyes (the manicured finger that only a Natural Mom can maintain, even while she grows her own organic food in the backyard). These books just confirm what we already suspected: we are (un)Natural Moms.

It even happens in church. Every Mother's Day we receive a flower and a reminder of the virtues of the Proverbs 31 woman. Natural Moms might experience a few proud moments when this mirror is held up in front of them, but those of us who can't sew, cook, or stay up all night have an especially tough Sunday.

An (un)Natural Mom is any mom who finds some everyday aspect of motherhood so challenging that she experiences shame, fear, or even despair. She sometimes wonders if she ever should have had children. She envies the seeming ease with which other moms navigate the parenting minefields. In spite of her best efforts, she experiences disappointment and disillusionment in herself as a mother.

It's time for a book that will give such a Christian mother a break. I need such a book. Perhaps I'm writing this for myself as much as for every other mom. My hope is that every mom will discover that God is a master designer who has made her to reflect something unique of Himself to the world. He has equipped her distinctly to be the perfect mom for the child or children she is called to raise.

Many years ago, before becoming a mom, I worked in private practice as a speech and language therapist and audiologist. I had a special interest in children with disabilities. Finding the key that led a six-year-old autistic child to utter his first words was one of the greatest thrills of my career. Week after week I tried what certainly was not a normal technique: I tried my utmost to frustrate him, believing that protest is the most basic form of communication. He never even grunted. One day, out of the blue, he turned and screamed at me, "Now you stop it!" The aggressive response was music to our ears. It had his mom and me in tears of joy. The key I used that day never worked on another autistic client. It was unique to him. I came to believe that when it comes to people, there is no size that fits all. With parenting as well, unique solutions are key.

In South Africa, where I live, we have eleven official languages, and in many of them one needs to be able to roll an *r* until it vibrates like a motorcycle engine! This is generally hard to learn in adulthood. The "program" for the pronunciation of an *r* is hardwired into the brain by then. Even if an adult reproduces the trilling sound successfully, when he or she tries to say it in a sentence, the brain defaults to the old program and the wrong sound comes out. My interest in brain injury led to a thesis on a new model for speech production. I used this knowledge to design therapy plans that could sneak through the back door of the brain so that adults could learn correct pronunciation without realizing what skills we were working on. The correct sound would just pop out one day and be there to stay.

My second belief about parenting flows from this experience with older articulation patients. The best way to unlearn ingrained habits and learn new ones is to bypass the obvious confrontation. The more you tell parents *not* to do what they have become accustomed to doing, the more despondent or resistant they become. But when they can construct a platform of success out of what they already do well, new skills come naturally.

The three parenting books I wrote before this one were the result of many such experiences with children and parents, as well as study, struggle, and prayers. My goal has always been to document the discoveries that could make life easier for (un)Natural Moms like me. I tested my findings by observing and teaching parents in various cultures. Parenting advice that worked in Europe did not necessarily appeal to parents in Africa. What I learned about potty training from parents in Ukraine horrified parents in North America. However, after trimming away the extremes and the traditions that may not have been as helpful as previous generations thought, I was left with some truths that I believe to be fairly universal.

These truths became the foundations of the Evergreen Parenting courses I teach with my team around the world. We work with the uniqueness of each family by using temperament profiling, temperament-specific parenting advice, and parenting-style summaries to help parents explore and use their own strengths. This approach offers a vast set of keys instead of one golden one. We realize that it's much harder to fix family issues than the pronunciation of *r*'s.

Judging by the evaluation forms returned to us by hundreds of parents each year, the temperament module in the course has had the most impact. It has introduced a new parenting language some parents now call Tree Talk. They are thrilled to discover that their uniqueness and their child's design can be sources of insights rather than fights. Their relational breakthroughs have validated the personality test behind your Tall Trees Parenting Profile.

Mothers are like trees: we grow through seasons of fruitfulness but also survive winters when everything seems bare and dead. We want to be the tree Psalm 1 speaks of, planted by living water, evergreen and fruitful, yet we sometimes wither a little. What makes us wither is different for each mom. The triggers that make us feel like a motherhood failure also vary greatly.

In this book we'll spend a day in the life of four different (un)Natural Moms. Their lives are connected, and their personalities both clash with and complement one another's. The four moms represent four strikingly different tree types: a perfectly pruned and punctual Boxwood Tree, a prickly but productive Rose Bush, a peace-loving and patient Pine Tree, and a playful and positive Palm Tree.

The unique beauty of each mom's mothering style encompasses her flaws as well as those traits that reflect God's heart. It is my hope that this book will help all moms discover an important truth: from crib to college send-off, even the mom who feels ill equipped for this important job is more than enough for her family. In fact, in Christ she is a (super)Natural Mom. A (super)Natural Mom is not perfect; she is perfectly content with making the best of the aspects of motherhood that God has gifted her with. She relies on the work of the Holy Spirit to enable her to grow in those aspects of motherhood that don't come to her naturally. Through her, God is writing a beautiful story into her household.

"Make a careful exploration of who you are and the work you have been given, and then sink yourself into that. Don't be impressed with yourself. Don't compare yourself with others. Each of you must take responsibility for doing the creative best you can with your own life" (Gal. 6:4–5).

With love and grace from an (un)Natural Mom,
Hettie Brittz

1

Confessions of an (un)Natural Mom

My first pregnancy and birth were textbook perfect: full-term, vaginal, and without any significant medical intervention. My prayers had been answered. My baby latched on three minutes after birth. I glowed with gratitude and pride. One would think I was a natural. I did.

In those days, South African health-care plans allowed for a three-day stay for screening tests and postnatal care, even after a complication-free birth. The shocking realization that I am an (un)Natural Mother hit home on day three. I noticed that my baby needed a bath, so I confronted the nurse the moment she stepped into the neonatal ward.

"So, when are you going to bathe the baby?" I asked. "She's already three days old! One would expect better care around here."

"Mrs. Brittz, she is *your* baby. You should have bathed her already—yesterday! One would expect you to know this." A particular look of disapproval accompanied this curt announcement by Nurse Napoleon. It was to be the first of many such looks.

I turned away as redness and shame washed over me. In the same way some children skip the chicken pox, I seemed to have skipped the moment when I was supposed to be endowed with mothering instincts. I glanced at the tiny, whimpering bundle in the crib next to me and feared for both of us. How could I have messed up before even taking my precious daughter home?

High Expectations and Unexpected Lows

I had longed to be a mom. My husband and I married young, and I wanted to wait a year or two before starting a family; he wanted to wait indefinitely. We agreed to wait five years. *Agreed* is perhaps an overstatement. I counted down the years and then the months. Nine months before the five-year mark, I poured him a strong cup of coffee and nonchalantly brought up the approaching deadline. A slight dispute over the meaning of "five years" ensued. He thought we had agreed to quit contraception at the five-year mark. I thought we had agreed I would quit double espressos by then, assuming a breastfed newborn would not appreciate a grande latte with an extra shot. After a serious talk, we agreed that I would stop taking the pill immediately and we would start trying to get pregnant at the five-year mark. *Agreed* is definitely an overstatement.

Month after month I fixed my drawn-out stare on home-testing dipsticks. I even dug them out of the trash just to inspect them one more time. Perhaps they needed just another minute—or a day— to show that second pink stripe and confirm the fulfillment of my dream. But it never happened.

Exasperated, my dear husband bought us a miniature dachshund puppy. Dog food is cheaper than monthly visits to the gynecologist, after all. We both poured all our affection on the little ratlike pup even before she grew fur and became somewhat likable. She slept between us.

And then, on a beautiful morning close to the six-year mark, two pink stripes appeared. My husband made up the house in streamers and balloons while I went to the doctor's office to confirm the result with a blood test. We were overjoyed. God had given me my heart's desire.

The pregnancy was a breeze. I felt guilty for dodging morning sickness, swelling, varicose veins, heartburn, and virtually every other pregnancy ailment in the book. Apart from putting on thirty-one pounds, pregnancy suited me like a second skin—without stretch marks. Doesn't that just scream Natural Mother? I assumed that motherhood itself would be this painless.

My studies as a speech pathologist and audiologist included three years' worth of psychology, early childhood development, neurology, anatomy, and physiology classes. I attended a complete series of prenatal classes with my hubby. I refused to attend the class about cesarean sections, vowing that I would give birth vaginally. After all, my mom had given birth to my older brother, me and my twin brother, and a fourth baby this way. Surely I would do the same.

We outfitted the baby room. I sewed the crib bumper and comforter, tiny pillowcases, curtains, and a wall-mounted diaper holder to blend in with the nursery's theme. I packed my hospital bag at seven months. How could I, in spite of all this preparation, stare at my unbathed baby without sensing the call to Natural Motherhood?

I resolved to do better and started doing everything by the book. My daughter slept through the night at six weeks. She was on a four-hour feeding routine during the day, as the biblical parenting book on the shelf prescribed, and I felt like the mom of the year for about two weeks, when I began to suspect she wasn't gaining enough weight.

Off I went to the expert for feeding advice. I invited a friend along for the expedition. She had concerns of her own. Her baby, who was three months older than mine, seemed to be gaining too much weight. *How could too much mother's milk ever be a problem?* I wondered. She breastfed like a Natural Mom. She was clearly not a rookie like I was. She had proven herself by keeping baby number one alive and well fed for two years and was excelling with her second, as far as I could tell.

The nurse we went to see was known far and wide. Her waiting room was packed. She looked like Mary Poppins to me with her tightly rolled gray bun pinned just perfectly on her wise head like a crown. The Baroness of Breastfeeding. I watched her meticulously weigh every baby as I moved closer and closer to the moment of truth. It was almost my turn. I could tell by watching the mothers' faces that although our babies were put on the scales, we were the ones being weighed. As a last, desperate attempt to hide the obvious malnutrition of my eight-week-old baby, I quickly fixed a small bottle of formula on the sly and fed her a few ounces.

"Kent!"

My friend stepped up. Her beautiful baby with chubby cheeks made quite the impression on both the scales and Mary Poppins, whose verdict was brutal.

"My goodness, look at these chubby legs! Not exactly beauty pageant material, are they? You have to slow down on the feeding, Mommy! Her skin can hardly hold her in!" I wanted to run. My friend did—out the door. I thought she may have cried a bit too. My model of Natural Motherhood had been gutted by a gray-haired lady who had, for all her qualifications, forgotten how vulnerable we were.

"Brittz!"

I bravely offered up my baby. Would the bony legs at least pass the test?

"Eight weeks? Are you breastfeeding? 'Cause if you are, stop it! This poor thing is starving. Give her a bottle, please! And give her something for this oral thrush as well. That means treat your nipples too!" She didn't even offer a spoonful of sugar to help this bitter medicine go down.

"It isn't thrush; it's formula milk!" I retorted. "I fed her some milk just now, and I suppose I didn't shake the bottle well enough to dissolve the powder properly. See, it wipes right off!"

The already speechless moms on the long row of chairs seemed to exchange their shame on my behalf for utter shock as they watched me stick unwashed fingers into my baby's mouth. My efforts to wipe off her tongue were futile.

"I know the difference between thrush and milk!" Mary Poppins hissed without even looking. There was the same stare Nurse Napoleon had given me. Do they teach this in nursing school?

I grabbed my scrawny baby and ran out, fearing more than ever that she'd be better off with a Natural Mom who could at the very least produce enough natural nourishment. Through the tears of bitter disappointment with my body, I vowed to stop at a pharmacy on the way home and buy every natural lactation remedy available to humankind. I also purchased a large supply of formula in case I was beyond medical help. Perhaps I wasn't a natural, but at least I was practical!

To increase my milk supply, I downed bottles of berry elixir, took a prescribed medication twice a day, and supplemented each meal with a special shake. Any of these should have produced a fountain of milk, but they all had only one effect on me: exponential expansion. I faced reality and broke out the plastic bottles and formula.

My baby turned out to be allergic to the first three types of formula we tried. She gagged on all but one type of silicone teat. Even with the aid of artificial milk, I failed. Helplessness overwhelmed me.

Our dachshund must have sensed what was going on. She beat me to the crib every time my baby daughter cried. One day I noticed that the dog's nipples were swollen and thought she must be expecting puppies. She wasn't fully grown yet, and we had no idea if the daddy dog was of a much larger breed. If so, her pregnancy could be fatal. Off to the vet we went. He examined her, smiled, and asked if another pet in the home had recently given birth. He had seen this phenomenon a few times in his career: some animals have a mothering instinct so strong that they will lactate for the orphaned offspring of other animals and act as wet nurses.

That did it for me: even my dog was more natural than I was. She sensed that my baby lacked a real mother! I cried for days, and for many reasons. Why was I nauseated every time I bent over the crib rail to pick up my daughter for her feeds? Why did I feel as though my life was over? Why did I love her to the point of being willing to die for her, while finding the daily baby-care chores unfulfilling? It didn't help that she had chronic colic for six months. It seemed like years.

None of This Comes Naturally for Me!

There was light in the tunnel. Joyce, our favorite babysitter, lived with us in an apartment separate from our main house. Her window faced the window of the baby's room. Joyce woke up more easily than I did and enjoyed diaper changes more than I did. By the time my daughter was ten months old, I hardly ever needed to get up early in the morning. I would wake up refreshed to find that Joyce had already changed my baby's diaper, fed her, dressed her up, and propped her up in a high chair or playpen with toys strewn around her. It was ever so convenient that I didn't object. I was home all day with my daughter, providing all of her needs until bedtime. My loving voice, singing a lullaby I wrote especially for her, was the last sound she heard every night. Letting Joyce be the first face she saw in the mornings couldn't do any harm, could it?

Two years later we had a son. He went past the due date by a full eight days and gave me my stretch marks: those purple badges of motherhood that turn silver with age. This time I walked out of the neonatal ward with a clean baby I had bathed without being told. Even the breastfeeding went smoothly. I ignored most of the how-to books on my bookshelf and tried to loosen up about motherhood. Was I finally a Natural Mom?

I was about to be told.

At this point in my career, I directed an after-school care center in a poor part of our city. The kids who attended were between seven and seventeen years old and consumed most of my attention. I fed them, helped them do homework and therapy, and walked some home to alcoholic parents and empty pantries. I was the person they called on when domestic violence became unbearable or when they simply needed lice shampoo. The brokenness of families and God's love for them stayed with me forever. Even when mothers asked me which one of their kids they should give up in order to be able to feed the rest, I had hope. God had put His hope in my heart.

My daughter tagged along as I labored to lead these kids and their families to Christ and a better future. But when she needed attention, she no longer called me Mommy; she called me Auntie

Hettie: the one who could see others' needs clearer than her own daughter's.

Her third assault on her baby brother with the intent to inflict grievous bodily harm (details withheld for the sake of protecting a minor) made a red flag fly high. My line of work offered me access to many professionals, so I contacted a play therapist who had a stellar reputation. Perhaps she could nip my toddler's criminal tendencies in the bud. I prayed she could. I was genuinely concerned.

We filled out forms, answered case-history questions, and waited while the therapist evaluated our daughter. At the end of their session, the therapist showed me our three-year-old's basic drawing of our household. She was in the middle between Joyce and her Daddy. Some distance away were her brother and me. I was nearly falling off the page.

"Your daughter is not disturbed. She has an insecure, ambivalent bond with you. You are nurturing her baby brother but not her. She resents that. That is the reason for her aggression toward him. She doesn't know who you want to be in her life—or if you even want to be her mother. Do you?"

Nurse Napoleon and Mary Poppins had caused me discomfort. This therapist inflicted searing pain.

I can't recall what I blabbered through my blubbering. I yearned to say, "Yes, I want to be her mommy!" but I also recognized the painful truth: though I was happy to go for walks in the park, play games on the floor, and think up creative educational games to play during bath time, I did not do what she needed the most when she needed it. I saw it then: I had given away precious bonding moments to Joyce because I didn't realize how short and sweet those moments were. Too little holding for no reason but love. Too little cuddling. Too little skin-to-skin.

The play therapist seemed to know all about me. She appeared to know my daughter better than I did as she started talking to me about the "evident temperament clash" she observed in our relationship.

"You are driven, hurried, and task oriented; your little girl is *so* laid back. Do you even hear how slowly she speaks? She's not as you described her on these forms you filled out. You think she is strong willed and oppositional, but she has just dug in her heels because you're moving so fast! You'll have to meet her where she is, not where you are. Tell me about bath time."

"I have her bathed, hair washed, and dressed in five minutes flat. Easy."

She gave me my bonding homework: I was to stay in the bath with my daughter for a minimum of half an hour, lathering her with foam, drawing pictures on her back with my finger and making her guess what they were. We were to take turns. We were to splash about without caring too much about getting the floor wet. I was to take my time to dry her off properly. I was to rub lotion all over her little body as if she were a newborn, because she craved this. And I was to dress her slowly and hold her until she let go first. I also needed to put together a little nurse's bag, complete with Band-Aids, M&M's (fake "pills"), and ointments to put on scrapes, cuts, and bruises—even mosquito bites. I was to find at least one reason daily to give this special care to her.

My inward knee-jerk response was *No way, I don't have time for all of that!* followed immediately by a covenant I knew I couldn't keep without God's help: *I will do this even if it kills me, and it probably will—in a good way. Lord, help me! None of this will come naturally for me!*

I went home equipped with a few copied pages from a book about temperament. I kept saying to myself, "I'm not stupid. I'm not ignorant. I'm not ungodly or uncaring. Why is motherhood so hard for me?" There had to be an easier way without all this aggravation and shame.

Mothering on the Road

When our daughter was four and our son eighteen months, my husband's band launched several ministry tours to Europe, Canada, and the United States. For three years in a row, our family spent four months, six months, and three months respectively touring with the band.

My motherhood was put to the ultimate stress test when our lives went on the road. There was little routine. Every day we lived from one strange home or cheap hotel to another, never knowing how long it would be to the next diaper-changing station or microwave oven. This unsettled existence shook my foundations. My kids were proof of that, especially my son.

On the second tour, at a high school in Iowa, I left my kids in the backstage room, where snacks for the band were laid out on platters. My daughter had art supplies to amuse herself with, and my son had a set of simple animal puzzles. (Who gives a little boy a puzzle and thinks he will behave for the next two hours? This (un)Natural Mom did.) I joined our host in the foyer, chatting away. She was a teacher at the school. Together we bemoaned the state of discipline in schools and Christian homes. I made the ignorant statement that South African parents still had a firmer grip on discipline than American parents. At this point she asked if it were time for me to check on my kids. I didn't think it was because, as I had pointed out already, we South Africans are not known for letting our kids run amok. She insisted. I relented.

The backstage room was a war zone. Ranch dressing and mustard splashes covered the floor. Cherry tomatoes, broccoli florets, and strawberries lay squashed everywhere. It was clear what the rules of the game had been: dip and demolish! My son was still stepping on tomatoes to send the juicy pulp squirting everywhere. Puzzles couldn't beat this!

My daughter froze at the sight of me and then offered a perfectly logical explanation: "I dropped one tomato and it popped and then we just couldn't stop." The food-fight demon had taken over their bodies, and it was not their fault.

After waking up the janitor so we could borrow his mobile cleaning unit, then cleaning up the room as well as we could, I sat down with my kids for a serious talk. I dished out what I considered to be fair punishment at the time but regretted later. We sorted what remained of the intact fruit and vegetables onto separate platters, and then I noticed it: the ranch dip was a light yellow color. *Perhaps Iowa has a yellow version*, I thought optimistically, or perhaps it was just a little mustard contamination that could be scraped off the top with a teaspoon. Instead, my investigation revealed a surprise of eight or ten large strawberries, which I hoisted hastily out of the dip. I gave the already-churned ranch dressing a good stir and wished the earth would open up and swallow me whole.

In the months to come, my son's misbehavior escalated to the point where I might have been locked up if not for the fortunate fact that we never stayed in any town long enough for people to blame me. Everyone probably thought my "poor boy" was just "having a bad day." My training should have kicked in; I was missing all the classic signs of severe sensory integration difficulties. Instead, all I saw was a naughty child I could not control no matter how hard I tried. He needed his home, stability, and occupational therapy.

(un)Natural Times Four

Toward the end of a long tour of "bad days," I started feeling off-color and suspected that I could be pregnant. I certainly was moody enough, but the home test kits kept coming up negative. My husband was convinced too. I had used swear words only twice before: during the first trimesters of both my previous pregnancies. As far as he was concerned, this third bout of bad language was irrefutable proof.

We were in Canada when the pregnancy test finally came up positive, and a former South African doctor even used a fetal ultrasound so we could hear our third baby's heartbeat. We were a little concerned about the circumstances and timing but grateful.

I visited my gynecologist as soon as we were back on South African soil. He stated that I was about eight weeks along. I knew that it was eleven or twelve. Four weeks later, he relayed that I wasn't more than ten weeks pregnant. Powerful denial stopped me from facing what should have been clear by then.

At about seventeen weeks, I woke up gloomy one morning—no physical symptoms, just sadness. When I called my doctor, he urged me to relax. Fears are normal, he said, and so are mood swings, but I should come in if I had cramps or bleeding. My husband was in Scotland at the time. I called my mom and asked her to take me to her doctor. I just knew I had lost my child, and I didn't want to face it alone.

The doctor placed the probe on my belly and we all saw it clearly: a few short strings of vertebrae hung together here and there, and buttony bones floated around in the cloudy amniotic fluid.

My mother wept and I tried to hold it together. I told the doctor about the negative pregnancy tests up to about eight weeks and the slow growth that I had ignored. He told me that a body could be in as much denial as a soul. My body just didn't want to let go of this child as it should have. It had let me down again, like with the breastfeeding. It had allowed something unnatural to occur inside of me. It had let my unborn baby down. I felt damaged.

The decomposition in my womb was serious. I was sent home immediately to pack a hospital bag. The assisted miscarriage and procedure that followed were unpleasant. So much tissue had to be removed that I was told another pregnancy might tear my womb and cause life-threatening internal bleeding. I would need to return for a hysterectomy after I had recovered.

I briefly mourned the loss of hope that I would have a third baby. Then I shoved the sadness deep down, as I tended to do with the sum of sad feelings about my many mothering failures, and moved on. I never went back for the operation.

Less than a year later, we were considering adopting an orphan of HIV/AIDS, having realized that an inability to bear children does not mean an inability to have and love them. I was compiling a scrapbook of our family for the baby's ailing mother. She was to choose which of three candidate families to give her baby to. My husband looked over my shoulder and said, "Hon, we make such beautiful babies. Why don't we just try once more? If your womb is as damaged as they say, the pregnancy just won't take, will it?"

And that is how I fell pregnant the fourth time. We bowed out of the adoption process, and I enjoyed another uneventful pregnancy. The concern of the initial presence of a large hematoma and that my womb could possibly tear dissipated as every examination showed a healthy mom and baby.

In the years that followed, I had many moments in which the disapproval of others and my own high standards plagued my mothering. At fourteen months old, my youngest discovered promethazine tablets, an antihistamine I used to help me sleep on long flights. The tablets were in a tightly closed pill bottle inside a paper packet, hidden in my passport pouch and zipped up in a handbag. They were hardly lying around, but she found them. She ate all ten of what resembled blue mini M&M's and escaped death only by God's miraculous healing power. Watching her drool and convulse, her arms flailing uncontrollably and eyes rolling back in her head for eight hours nonstop, I knew I would never forgive myself if my carelessness caused her any permanent harm. A nurse in the pediatric ICU must have been thinking the same thing because she gave me another look to add to my collection.

Health and wellness was clearly not my strong area. My son came walking into our room one night wheezing like a chain smoker. Once admitted to the hospital, oxygen mask over his face, we were given the diagnosis: asthma. I was surprised that a child could get his first asthma attack at age nine. When I interviewed him about parenting failures to list in this book, he said, "Mom, I didn't have my first asthma attack that day. Do you remember when we had that tour where I coughed so much? It was when we spent Christmas in Atlanta and you tied the tinsel around me as if I were a Christmas tree? Well, I felt exactly the same almost every day of that tour. I told you I couldn't breathe. You thought it was just a bad cough. You never even took me to the doctor!" He was four then. This (un)Natural Mom had a son with asthma and missed it for five years.

When he was ten, his father and I had a silly fight about gift wrap. We ended the disagreement, and my husband went out to buy fast food because the fight had happened in lieu of cooking dinner.

At seven that night, we discovered that our son was not in the house. After an hour of searching even dresser drawers and every hiding place in the already dark garden, we had to face the reality that our son had left our yard. It was freezing outside.

In South Africa, many middle-class neighborhoods are enclosed and have gated security. I insisted that the security guard search every car going out, fearing that our son might have been kidnapped. I prayed one prayer over and over again as we searched for four hours: "Lord, whatever is happening to my child right now, be near him. Your presence makes all the difference. Be bigger than whatever could frighten him. His days are in Your Book. You have the keys to life and death. Only You can come and get him. But please, Lord, don't let it be today."

With the help of neighbors whose questions were embarrassing to answer, we combed the entire fenced community and then the reeds next to the river that runs through it. We were piercing the dark water with flashlights when a neighbor called to say he had found our son in a dangerous floodplain known for its vagrants, curled up in his sleeping bag with the drawstring pulled tight above his head, fast asleep. He had set off armed with only an extra pair of socks and a sleeping bag. (At least he had taken my advice to think ahead. I would have been proud had I not been scared out of my mind.)

As I carried my son home on my back, as we do in Africa, even my unspeakable relief could not stop me from explaining how embarrassed I was to have unnecessarily summoned the police dogs.

I don't think he felt bad about it though. I think his eyes lit up at the thought of being sniffed out by the canine unit!

Now my oldest daughter is seventeen. She is well fed but still skinny and can probably add several episodes to this story of my less-than-stellar mothering skills. Fortunately, she is too kind to do so. She has forgiven me for many offenses, such as accidentally booking a moving truck on her tenth birthday. (We shared a milk tart from the nearest supermarket among cardboard boxes, then sent her off to the ice-skating rink with a friend so that we could complete the move. Shame on us!) We now bathe separately but still have the bond that was forged among the soapsuds. She has made me more natural and keeps doing it each year.

Our youngest daughter refuses to be a victim of an (un)Natural Mom. She tells me how it is done and makes sure I do it. When it's been too long since her last bedtime story, mom-and-daughter date, evening swim, or cuddle in mom's bed, she lets me know and schedules an opportunity for me to redeem myself. She too has changed me.

My son wants me to add just one more thing: I can't cook or bake to save anyone's life. He does see the bright side to everything though. "Mom, since we aren't used to fancy food, we're always the kids at church camp who love the food! It makes us seem grateful, and that makes you look good!"

Just the Right Kind of (un)Natural

I believe that God hears my silent prayers for assurance every now and then. I am confident He still wants me on this job—that He still has me penned into His purposes as the Plan A mother to these three eternal souls (plus the little one I'll meet in heaven). He has answered these prayers so I can see a unique and beautiful connection between who I am and who my children need as a mother, in spite of my mistakes. My dreamy daughter needs the occasional push; my strong-willed son needs me to lay down the law; my youngest needs me to stay out of the kitchen so that she can operate there, which suits us both well.

Affirmation of my being the right mom for my kids came to me a few years ago on a very dark night. Known as the mom who had all three of her children trained to sleep in their own cribs by six weeks, I was often made to feel bad by mothers who regarded this as unnatural. In South Africa, as in other parts of the world, many parents place a high value on bonding with their children in a family bed. This is considered critical to a child's lifelong emotional well-being. My peers never criticized me directly, but their stories did. What they said made sense to me but contradicted the books I regarded as my parenting bibles. This unnerved me. What if they were right about their own children as well as mine? What if training my kids to sleep in their own rooms, in the dark, doors closed, would prove to be a mistake in the long run?

One night four armed robbers breached our gated neighborhood and climbed through an open window into our house. They tied up my husband and me at gunpoint, took us through the house while gathering all the valuables, and even kidnapped my husband. I became a South African rape statistic. God's comforting presence and a number of reassuring miracles during that night kept us alive and intact. My husband was able to make his way back home unharmed. Sleep trained and in their own bedrooms, all three of our children slept through the entire ordeal. They woke up at seven the next morning while the police were dusting the house for finger-prints. Had they slept in our room, they would have witnessed what children shouldn't see.

Perhaps, besides the obvious gracious intervention by God, my (un)Natural mothering style made a difference to our family that night and in the months that followed—an important difference. The nightmare of what had happened was, to my children, like any other nightmare. They were used to being comforted in their own beds, never doubting that they were safe even away from us, even in the dark. They went back to sleeping in their own rooms and beds from the first night we were allowed back in our home, a mere three days later.

Somewhere on the other side of the world is a mom who praises God that she had all her children in her bed with her when an unexpected tornado hit their town. She was able to get them all to safety, thanks to her parenting preference. Had she been the mother of my household, with kids spread out in three bedrooms, she might have had to choose which child to save. Her relief is the same as mine. She might have been told that she was a bad mother for not training her kids to sleep in their own beds. Like me, she now knows there is not just one way that works for everyone. God has given her unique grace.

I choose to believe and will continue to make the case that each (un)Natural Mom is exactly the right kind of unnatural. Her design fits the design of her children. In spite of her unique, unnatural bits and pieces, she is preparing her family for a journey only God knows everything about. Let all other mothers and nurses and even Mary Poppins be silent and observe the wonder of the (un)Natural Mom.

For Reflection

1. When was the first time you felt out of your depth as a mom?

2. The author confesses to several aspects of being (un)Natural (trouble with breastfeeding, ambivalence toward bonding and cuddling, not fond of baking and sewing). Are you a Natural in any of these areas? Have you ever celebrated those mothering strengths as gifts?

3. Has a "Nurse Napoleon" or "Mary Poppins" or anyone else ever made you feel ashamed of your mothering? How has the judgment of others affected your confidence?

4. What is your greatest disappointment about mothering? Your greatest joy?

5. Do you believe that God chose you to be the mother your kids need? Why or why not?

2

The Counterfeit Call
to Be "Natural"

Generations of mothers are passing on the family quilt and silver tea-spoon collection along with ideas that make many moms feel entirely inadequate. Myths have crept into our collective motherhood narrative like moths into a hope chest. Modern mothers keep adding new demands to the old list of standards without crossing out some things that need to go. When these demands are not clearly written in the Word of God, they often fall into the category of man-made rules that become crushing burdens. I am sure this growing list begs for some editing.

Throughout the ages, women have had to prove their chastity by bleeding on the honeymoon sheet (even though not all virgins bleed), their fertility by having sons soon after marriage (even though we now know that men are responsible for the male chromosomes), and their womanhood by being fulfilled by motherhood alone. Talk about a bar set high!

I intend to purge seven myths from the hope chest that I will someday pass on to my daughters and maybe even a daughter-in-law. These issues may be only mine, but I'm breaking out the mothballs anyway.

Myth #1: Every Woman Must Be Naturally Maternal

One of the frowns in my collection came in my late teens, when I was looking for ways to earn extra money. I chose vacuum packing cheese and weighing cold cuts in the supermarket deli over babysitting. Why would a "normal" young woman prefer to take inventory of perishables instead of honing her mothering skills among the bibs and baby blankets in a nursery? If asked this question in so many words, I could have given many reasons, but they wouldn't have led anywhere. Who would believe that raw chickens needing to be skewered for the rotisserie oven felt more urgent to me than a baby bottle needing to be refilled? Even before we are old enough to marry and be mothers, we are often expected to have our eyes on that milestone. I didn't, and I know I'm not alone.

Theodore Roosevelt is quoted in *The World's Famous Orations, Volume 10, America III* as having said the following about women who do not have motherhood as their primary aspiration:

> The existence of women of this type forms one of the most unpleasant and unwholesome features of modern life. If anyone is so dim of vision as to fail to see what a thoroughly unlovely creature such a woman is I wish they would read Judge Robert Grant's novel *Unleavened Bread*, ponder seriously the character of Selma, and think of the fate that would surely overcome any nation which developed its average and typical woman along such lines.
> Unfortunately it would be untrue to say that this type exists only in American novels.[1]

These words were said in 1905. Remnants of this viewpoint still exist more than a hundred years later, couched in subtler phrases. The woman who aspires to things outside of married life and motherhood is often left out in the cold. If she openly postpones her child-rearing years, she may be urged to attend a course at church to correct her thinking. Of course, if her decision is the result of pain from her own childhood or fears about the future, a biblical course may be the best investment in her healing and freedom. Still, little space is left for the possibility that something other than mothering could be God's Plan A for her.

Instead of being guided and mentored to readiness, she may hear that marriage is primarily for reproduction, a belief that can invalidate her God-given sexuality. But what about the possibility that marriage is ultimately a mysterious and wonderful covenant that mirrors the union between Christ and his bride, the church? From this metaphor, we can mine new meaning and pure examples of love, intimacy, sacrifice, companionship, and delight. Marriage is preparation for the wedding feast to come, and a childless marriage can beautifully portray many eternal truths.

A married woman who delays motherhood might be guided to do so by God for reasons others might not see. In His sovereign knowledge of all that awaits us, God might graciously take her through a challenge before adding the responsibility of child rearing to her life. Some women are relieved their children were not born before they discovered that aggressive tumor or their spouse's infidelity—crises that demanded their full attention and would have been infinitely more difficult to navigate with a baby on one's hip.

The pregnant teen or the never-married mom might find herself in a special Siberia. Some Christians will disqualify her from being part of the bride of Christ. Her children may be declared "under the curse" and labeled "unplanned," as if God writes the life stories of only some but not others. I have to plead that we at least owe her this mercy: to allow her to identify with scared and shaken Mary, the Hebrew teen in an age of stoning, pregnant out of wedlock with a baby she could not explain. (She's the only teen who could honestly say, "I don't know how it happened. We didn't do anything.") Like Mary, any untimely mom has to submit to God eventually and find her own way of singing, "The Mighty One has done great things for me—holy is his name" (Luke 1:49 NIV).

Married women who intend to delay or avoid motherhood, but find God has other plans, face their own challenges. A mom once introduced her daughter to me as The-Surprise-Gift-Courtesy-of-Heel-Balm-That-Contained-Antibiotics. Before we judge her, we should wonder what a shock it must have been to get pregnant when her only goal was softer feet. Had she known that the antibiotics would render her contraceptive ineffective, she may have chosen cracked heels. Of course, if approached with tenderness and understanding, she might come to credit God's perfect provision, and not the heel balm, for her beautiful daughter!

Many women need to know it's okay to wait until they feel emotionally ready to have children. When such moms are gently and patiently guided through their insecurities, the wait will be worth it. If they're bamboozled into motherhood, it will be too easy to blame others when difficulties arise. Those mentored with realistic expectations are more likely to embrace even the darker days.

Myth #2: Every Mom Must Get Pregnant Naturally

"But I *am* maternal!" some women will exclaim. "I want a baby so much it hurts. It's just not working out for me."

This is where all the Hannahs of the Bible (1 Sam. 1–2) and of today get branded *unnatural* before their mothering journey even begins. From what I have seen and heard, the hormones used during assisted procedures can drive a woman fairly close to insanity. The process is anything but natural, though it is all in the service of nature. Then the great cost, the wait, the stress, the spike of joy at the pulsing image on the ultrasound screen, and the breathless anticipation while a second, third, or even fourth beating heart is counted. Then more waiting, more painful procedures—and still no guarantee. Only God can call life out of our mortal and manufactured matter.

In our first years of mothering, my best friend and I shared baby news regularly, especially sad news. During her second honeymoon, she stepped on a stonefish in Mauritius. A spine became lodged in her heel bone and sent toxins through her body, leading to an immediate miscarriage after the trip and several since. She was in the doctor's office when I called to announce I was pregnant with our third baby. It was a year after her last unsuccessful assisted-reproduction procedure, but since then she had miraculously become pregnant naturally with twins. We would be pregnant together! Before I could tell her the wonderful news, she told me she had started bleeding that morning, rushed to her doctor's office, and arrived with just the one baby still showing signs of life. I stayed on the phone with her as she watched the heaving white heart-blob in the center of the other twin's tadpole body. Within seconds all movement stopped. I left the news about my pregnancy for later.

She went on to have two more babies but lost count of the miscarriages in between. She is the bravest (un)Natural Mom I know. She stands tall among women who have experienced much shame and pain—women whose bodies finally behave naturally as well as those whose never do.

The confrontation with the fact that one's body has something wrong with it, so that what is supposed to happen spontaneously just doesn't happen, is excruciating. Even if the trouble isn't in her own body, a woman tends to feel responsible. Some women admit they don't enjoy trying for a baby anymore. Childhood dreams of motherhood can begin to show cracks after someone has been subjected too long to something so unromantic and medically complex.

Unfortunately, this honest pain can evoke sermons that add insult to injury. If a woman seems to try too hard, she might be told that motherhood clearly isn't meant to be; if she gives up when it becomes too hard or expensive, she might be accused of lacking faith.

I have known mothers of every temperament type to go through the valley of childlessness. Each traverses the terrain differently, and each is criticized by moms who have different natures. But our individual designs predictably explain why one mom gives up, another never mourns the miscarriages, and a third chooses to approach a surrogate. The initial myth—that there is something wrong with a mother who can't conceive naturally—expands to suggest that whatever a woman does to deal with her pain is also wrong somehow.

I pray that these Hannahs never have to deal with the artless answers offered by well-meaning but sometimes ignorant mothers:

- If you can just relax, it will happen in good time.
- God must feel you're not ready.
- Perhaps there is a curse of infertility on your family's bloodline that you haven't broken.

Some of these admonitions may be true, but oh, how much it hurts when others speak words that add to our feelings of inadequacy!

The mom who chooses the adoption route, whether she can or cannot conceive a baby, experiences a pregnancy of its own kind. The approval by the adoption agency may be her "double pink stripe." Instead of ultrasounds, she goes in for visits at the orphanage in Africa. Her pregnancy can last for years. She also has a readied room, a baby bag by the door, and a supply of formula. Her waters break when the adoption agency finally calls with good news. This unnatural pregnancy is supernatural in my book.

Myth #3: Every Mom Must Give Birth Naturally

The list of natural-birth boxes for an expectant mother to tick seems to have grown exponentially since I took prenatal classes. We had just two options: vaginal or cesarean section. You could be proud of yourself if you opted for the first. You were hailed as heroic and felt a sense of cave-woman pride. If you could forgo the spinal epidural or narcotics drip as well, you were even higher up the gauge of guts.

By my second pregnancy, I had gathered many opinions from Natural Mothers, whose circle I gained access to because my daughter had been born without the aid of drugs. They didn't need to know that a phobia of needles was the reason and not my bravery or commitment to all things natural. These moms must have thought I was ready for the next level. I was encouraged to tear naturally rather than have an episiotomy. Tear naturally? So that my chances of being naturally incontinent would be higher? They were serious. Also, they suggested that a water birth was a much more natural experience. I should ask for that option and include family members. This was where I said something that got me dismissed permanently from this league of Natural Moms.

By my third pregnancy, I had figured out a few more helpful natural advantages. I was ready to imitate ancient nations in selected respects. I was not going to lie down as I did the first time but instead harness gravity and cooperate with nature by remaining upright until the baby threatened to fall out. Being the competitive type, I wanted to improve my record. The first birth took thirteen hours, the second seven. My goal was to more than halve that to three hours max. I walked briskly up and down the corridors with my doula on my heels. (Do I get one naturalness credit for having a doula?) She lifted my hospital gown every now and then for inspection until I literally had to be picked up onto the bed to give maybe three pushes in total. New record—check!

But some degrees of natural are just beyond me. I recently stumbled upon a blog with the title "I Regret Eating My Placenta." Apart from being something I can imagine one regretting, it seemed worth reading just to answer the nagging question "What?!" To my surprise, one can eat it raw, cooked, or powdered and turned into capsules. Several celebrities have done it. It is supposed to have anti-depressant and blood-health benefits. According to the article, it was the last stage of a truly natural birth. I had to concede that it doesn't get more natural than that.

Does the extremely natural birth plan make one more natural than the mom who had everything planned but was woken up by her water breaking at twenty-seven weeks? Is she unnatural if she has to have a cesarean section to save a baby who had the cord wrapped twice around his neck? Was I more natural than the mom whose baby was simply too bulky and had to have his shoulder broken, resulting in his collarbone sticking into his little lung, nearly killing him? Is this process not all beyond our control? Is it not just by grace that some of us have a so-called "natural birth" with no medical interventions?

There can even be grace in not putting your household through a natural home birth. I am convinced that if I had birthed any of my babies in a bath at home, there would have been casualties among the spectators. For example, my son can't even look at raw tomatoes without being nauseated. Considering all that motherhood demands of a mother, is it so wrong if she opts for something as close to her definition of *painless* and as far from her idea of *dramatic* as possible? Does it make her a bad mother if she selects a cesarean because she hates surprises, fears an out-of-control process, and has a husband who works on an oil rig and desperately wants to plan his time onshore around the birth?

Every mom's nature and life story call for a special birth. Should your nature call for all things natural and earthy, you should by all means go that route. If needles and white hospital sheets would spoil the day, then you should be free to find a way around those. The less we deny ourselves the choices that suit our personalities and resist the ways our bodies give birth, the better the memories of those important days when we enter into motherhood. I am convinced that the inclusion of a diversity of birth stories in the Bible, of which Jesus's may have been the most uncomfortable, makes it clear that God does not prescribe some culturally dictated notion of the ideal birth. Neither should we.

Myth #4: Every Mom Must Be a Natural at Breastfeeding (and Continue for as Long as Possible)

It still is one of the yardsticks with which mothers measure one another. We make all sorts of inferences about the duration of breast-feeding. The mom who starts off with the bottle right away tops the list of criminals. We feel she robs her baby of health advantages and is probably selfish. We forget that the reasons for not breastfeeding are as diverse as the moms themselves. A mother who contracted HIV through a blood transfusion would be selfish if she did breastfeed her baby, for example. And when a mother needs to take medication that could harm her baby, the bottle is the only option.

Harsh judgment in this department also goes to the mom who doesn't pump milk for her child when she returns to work, instead weaning the baby in advance. But not all employers support breast-feeding mothers. Also, not all mothers have the ability to do quality work while being interrupted every few hours to pump milk. Some do. The wisdom to know yourself and what you can sustain is crucial.

There is an assumption, on the other hand, that the mother who wears her baby and feeds on demand for the first two or even three years of her baby's life is selfless, the ultimate Natural Mother. I certainly do hold these moms in the highest regard. Many truly believe extended breastfeeding to have undeniable health benefits. They enjoy the physical closeness with their babies and toddlers. Some, on closer acquaintance, will admit to many insecurities in other areas. Some don't know how to wean and don't have the heart to ever let their children cry. They don't sleep well, feel trapped, and want their bodies back.

The bonding and health benefits of breastfeeding are supreme, yet we seem to forget that bonding is not just biological and physical and that health depends on so much more than what we digest in the first years of life. Attachment is an emotional and even spiritual process that can take place in many ways. It can even be repaired later in life if it did not fully form in infancy. The mom's frame of mind, facial expressions, subtle moods, and stress levels often play a larger role than the actual feeding method in establishing a loving attachment. That is why adoptive moms can bond just as well with their children as birth mothers.

How the attachment forms is also affected by the baby's temperament. Not all babies enjoy constant physical touch, after all. Although my eldest daughter needed more than I naturally gave, my son needed less than I wanted to give. (Bathing with him would have been the worst idea. His sensory issues made bath times his enemy. It would have been bond destroying!) In both cases, I had to understand my own nature and theirs in order to make the bond secure.

The La Leche League, a nonprofit organization that promotes breastfeeding, has a long line outside its doors. Blogs and websites for breastfeeding moms abound. Postnatal classes and follow-up visits to the clinic nurse are dominated by questions that contain terms such as *foremilk/hindmilk balance* and *the football position*. If breastfeeding were as natural as they say, we would not need all these terms, tools, and teachers, would we? Let's just admit that even this basic action is complex. The more we are told that anyone can breastfeed, the more helpless we feel when we struggle. An approach that allows for all biologies, allergies, life stories, and affinities would be such a relief to (un)Natural Mothers like me.

Myth #5: Every Mom Must Be a Natural Homemaker

A pastor and his wife once hosted our family while we were traveling in England. They had two kids and stood there in church in a tight bundle that just screamed "close-knit nuclear family." The mom was the most content woman I had ever seen. She was also the keen observer who noticed the first signs of my looming miscarriage. She gently insisted that I go home to South Africa to rest but didn't say why. She hugged me, and even though we were roughly the same age, I felt mothered. She had dog hair on her sweater.

When the pastor opened the door of their home, I quickly gave my kids the forbidding owl eyes and pursed lips that say, "Not a word!" Magazines and newspapers, puzzle boxes, and board games were stacked on every level surface and laced the walls all the way around the living room. Even the stairs had items stacked on both sides of every step, leaving just enough free space to step in the center. Dog hair everywhere confirmed that vacuuming had been out of the question for quite some time.

The dining room table held a gigantic sugar bowl, a gallon of long-life milk, a supply of clean bowls, and maybe five boxes of assorted cereal. Dirty dishes rose in a tall tower beside the kitchen door. When invited into the kitchen to be shown where we could prepare our own breakfast the next morning, I understood: there simply was no space for the dirty dishes inside.

Every counter, both sinks, the lid of the trash can, and three of the four stove burners were covered. Heaven forbid one should accidentally turn on the wrong burner! (Or maybe someone should. The kitchen begged for a brand-new start.) While pointing to the one burner and then to the eggs and bacon in the fridge, the friendly pastor took a new pan from its box, plopped it onto the stove, and said, "There you go!" I'm sure it was impossible to get to the used pan to wash it.

Back in the living room, our hostess had one child in her lap and one curled up next to her, giggling. She got up only once to show us to our bedrooms. It was clear they weren't freshly made, but she gave us the warmest invitation to sleep anywhere.

At the time, my daughter occasionally still needed a night diaper, but being an (un)Natural Mom, I forgot to take maximum precautions. I will admit here in writing that when she woke up to a wet bed, and I to morning sickness, I gave the damp bed one dismissive look, hugged my daughter warmly, and said, "Sweetie, it's quite all right. Nobody will notice." I bagged the wet pajamas to be washed in the next town and added the damp sheets to the overflowing laundry basket. I'm convinced the loving mom of this house would have done the same thing.

One could easily judge her, but a closer look at the stacks of apparent laziness would reveal worn-out children's books she clearly read as many times as the kids wanted to hear them, educational toys with sticky fingerprints that told of free exploration and ample playtime, and board games with the rules scribbled on the outside, revealing that she actually cared more than one would think. Every child's favorite bowl was in the clean stack on the dining room table. Looking where one really should be looking—in those children's faces—the primary evidence of their mother's love was clear as day: they looked like purring kittens.

Remembering this home always helps me feel a little better about not being a housewife of note. I rarely cook. All two electric stove plates and four gas burners are exposed at my house. The counters are almost bare. My friends, upon seeing the huge stove and oven after we moved in, almost without exception exclaimed, "Aaaagh, what a waste!"

There comes a time to face it, if you are one of us. Look at yourself in the mirror and think of something you can do really well, such as, *I can identify seven types of garden bird.* Say it out loud, followed by the bold admission "I'm not a great homemaker." Repeat until the urge to go for choux pastry, pasta making, wedding-cake baking, cross-stitching, tailoring, and macramé classes dissipates. I am not suggesting you intentionally try to be the opposite of the Proverbs 31 woman; rather, I advocate contentment with who you are. Then, if you choose to learn a skill that will serve your family, it will come from a place where what you offer gives life and love.

I descend from a long line of seminatural homemakers who have each found a few worthy dishes, clothing patterns, and crafts that serve their families well. It doesn't hurt to find at least one hot meal, one dessert, and one baked goodie you can actually produce fairly consistently, just to grant your children that essential wistfulness when they're in college (or married to an even more clueless cook) and say, "How I miss my mom's homemade food!" No need to overachieve. Sincere love and an emotional haven are worth so much more than a perfect house and a gourmet meal, though at times I still wish I had it in me to provide all four.

As for those who enjoy cooking from scratch and take pleasure in seeing a piece of fabric become an outfit or decoration, their children are fortunate to have them as moms.

Myth #6: Every Mom Must Find Parenting Natural

I have an email from an (un)Natural Mom. She has three degrees listed in her designed signature. Her writing has impeccable grammar and spelling. Yet she poses a question that reveals just how completely stumped she is by the daunting task of parenting a three-year-old girl: "Is it wrong to still have a story at bedtime even though she misbehaved this morning?"

This is a woman who can accurately predict the change in size of an international steel order of millions to the nearest hundred if she agrees to a 16 percent discount instead of 14 percent. This is a woman who flies to China on her own to negotiate deals with people who don't speak English. She never asks for help. Her gut tells her all she needs to know. But when it comes to her child, her gut is silent. She'd like someone next to her on her daughter's bed giving advice about whether to read *Goldilocks and the Three Bears* tonight.

This mom is embarrassed, judging by her apology at the end of her email "for asking such a silly question." Is she doomed? Are her kids? I believe not. I believe she knows when to guess, when to trust her gut, when to ask doctor Google, and when to log on to a parenting portal. There should be no shame in occasionally feeling lost. She's a natural at finding solutions, after all.

Eyewitnesses in my home have seen me look up issues in the alphabetical index of parenting books *I wrote*, looking for what I once knew were possible answers to everyday parenting problems. It's common knowledge that your first baby takes half your brain cells and your second the rest. I had three babies. I need reminding. Reading what I wrote years ago sometimes blows what's left of my mind.

I've always had trouble turning knowledge into practiced skill. Moms like me should be encouraged to keep asking for wisdom, which is far supreme to information. Our slowness in learning the art of motherhood should not be held against us. Isn't it wonderful that in the Bible, James tells us God's response to our many questions will never be "Shouldn't you know this by now?" This is what I understand James 1:5 to mean.

Myth #7: Every Mom Should Keep All Things Unnatural Away from Her Family Table

I confess that I am not a health-food fanatic. I once tried a diet that did not allow margarine, refined carbs, or any sugar or preservatives. I scared my teens when they watched videos taken of me in those years: "Mom, is that you? You look like a boy. Everything's like, uh, flat!" Only women who share my issues with certain body dimensions will understand how utterly blissful those words made me feel, but I also reached an important conclusion: not all natural eating leads to a natural body.

Perhaps not all "natural" eating leads to natural parenting, either.

Natural has become a word that, when stuck on a product label, kicks sales into the next bracket. Add "100% Natural" and, well, you may just have an item that flies into mothers' baskets all by itself—right next to the zero-additive natural fruit juice; the stone-ground, unbleached, GMO-free wheat bread; and the organically grain-fed, free-range, skinless chickens.

Call me a cynic, but I just don't think the words *natural* and *organic* automatically mean something is all good. Every time someone wants to sell me something 100 percent natural in exchange for an item already in my basket, they try to convince me that the chemicals in my food will kill me. I should read the list of unpronounceable ingredients on the back of the guacamole jar to see for myself why the poisonous stuff has a shelf life till doomsday. Their organic product, on the other hand, will be much better for me, even though it will probably start going bad as I walk out of the store since it has absolutely nothing but avocado in it. Whenever this happens, I have an urge to ask, "So it is completely natural? As natural as snake venom and marijuana?" If I'm in a really bad mood, I might want to ask if she's ever had teeth extracted naturally or if she'd like to go back to the age before razors and hair remover and embrace a jungle of natural body hair. I've never used any of this ammunition, though, because I know that the heart behind wanting to give me better-quality food is sincere.

No mom should be approached in the church aisle by a mother who wants to sell her a more natural way of mothering—not any more than a mom should be stopped in the grocery aisle to be sold a more natural jar of guacamole. I did not become defensive about my grocery choices from a single confrontation with one who stands for all things natural. My stance is a reaction to many unsolicited and often unfounded assaults by those who make food rules into spiritual laws in spite of Paul's appeal not to do so (Rom. 14:2–3).

Between my husband and me, we have passed on to our children every genetic marker for most forms of attention deficit hyperactivity disorder. They have displayed every ADHD symptom, from the dreamy kind to the run-around-the-house-so-fast-you-look-like-a-picket-fence kind. Of course we started our attempts to treat this with a natural approach, which included more love, more routine, more exercise, more therapy, less sugar and preservatives, limited screen time, and expensive natural supplements. It seemed to be working for our daughters, but not for our son. After many years of very little progress, we took the unpopular medicinal route. To this day, I count this experience as the biggest parenting mistake I have ever made (not the medication but the leaving it as a last resort).

I had avoided a pharmaceutical solution because I was told by an internationally acclaimed Christian speaker that medicine would permanently lock demonic water spirits into my son's brain. I was told he would become a drug addict in later life. I was told he would escalate from needing one tablet to needing handfuls to control all the various side effects. I was never told to pray and go with what God led me to do.

Thanks to the writings of Christian doctors in this field, and a brilliant pediatrician, I was able to put the facts behind these misconceptions—and behind some horrific true stories—into perspective. Contrary to what I was warned, our son takes only one capsule per day for his ADHD; has caught up on the delays caused by the condition; has gained emotionally, socially, and physically; and is hungry for God and not filled with demonic water spirits. He once said it well: "Mom, the meds just give me a step back and a second or two to make an intentional choice to act like myself."

My husband and I appreciate that many parents disagree with giving their kids unnatural substances, even medicines, in order to be natural. Blessed are those who never have to. That too is grace.

My family's health is important to me, and I believe that every mom should have her family's physical well-being on her heart. Health is broader than food, though, and includes adequate exercise, limited screen activity, time outdoors, rest and good sleep, a clean environment—the list goes on and on. Every mom can do only so much.

We appreciate the large number of parents who are passionate about ensuring healthful habits and nutritional eating in their own families without pressuring others to copy them.

The trending emphasis on organic food stems from well-founded concerns, but it is often beyond one's budget. When someone makes something into a gospel truth but it happens to be bad news to the poor, I always wonder, *If so many people live on less than I do, how can the organic-food message be the parenting equivalent of the good news?*

You might wonder what any of these myths have to do with temperament and parenting styles. The passing on of these myths—or the resistance to them—has everything to do with temperament. It is a certain personality that makes rules and loves them. It is a certain personality that prescribes them to others. It is a certain temperament that believes in myths and accepts the bondage they bring. It is a certain personality that rebels against anything that even looks like a one-size-fits-all blueprint (yes, I confess!), and yet another that read the beginning of this chapter and then moved on. Remember how you felt reading the chapter, because your reaction is part of your natural design. It is also an important part of breaking free and setting others free so that we can each walk our own journey with authenticity.

For Reflection

1. Have you ever believed any myths of motherhood? Which have especially made you doubt yourself? (It might be a myth not covered in this book.)

2. Think about a mom you know and admire. In what ways do you feel like you should be more like her?

3. Think about a mom you've judged because her parenting choices are different from yours. Why do you think mothers judge each other?

4. Was there anything in this chapter that challenged a belief you hold about motherhood? How might your experience as a mom change if you let go of that belief?

5. Which truth about mothering would you want to pass on to the next generation?

3

Your Own Kind of Natural

Motherhood has a way of bringing us to our knees, doesn't it? When we're desperate, we run to God. We all become more natural when we have God's help, but He doesn't seem to give us all the same guidance about our children. Why not?

To begin with, we don't ask the same questions. The places where her makeup melts and she can't pretend she's coping are unique to every mom. One mom might hear God say she should stop doing the very thing He told me to start doing! We both hear God. He seems to have more than one parenting book at hand to meet the needs of more than one kind of parent. If we are to give godly advice to fellow mothers, we may want to remember how God does it and put away our "One Way" guides.

Consider a few great mothers I know. One had her first baby at twenty and feels she could have started even earlier; another had her first baby at thirty-four and is still coming to terms with the loss of her youth. The third mom has four children and would easily raise seven, while the fourth feels that her household crossed the line from home to zoo once baby number three arrived. These moms are different in every other way: hair color, type of intelligence, favorite comfort food, amount of makeup applied when camping. How could they possibly be expected to embrace the same mothering style?

My fellow mothers, lined up in my mind like this, are similar to the trees planted in my backyard. They are each beautiful in their own right. They bloom differently. Some are stronger on the foliage side than on the flowering side. Some are fruit bearing, and others are fairly bare for most of the year. My family planted each one for a different reason: some for shade, some to be a barrier between us and the neighbors, some to be colorful in spring and others to brighten up fall. If we were to remove any one of them, there would be a gaping hole in a really well-balanced garden.

Could God be gardening in the same way? What if we moms are just like trees: 100 percent natural and yet diverse in our beauty? I have believed this to be true for a long time, and I have studied these differences. The day after the honest therapist confronted me with the truth about the clash between my nature and my daughter's, I started reading stacks of books about personality styles and temperament. The uncomfortable feeling of being labeled could not outweigh the relief I felt to learn something new about myself. I was not the only one who did things this way, cried about those things, and found certain activities utterly unfulfilling. I was normal! But the labels used to describe my personality type in these books irked me. I didn't want to be named after bodily fluids or animals. But then again, these books do accurately point out that my type tends to be easily offended and critical.

The word *temperament* literally means "mixture." We are blends of traits and genes. Our blood types are fixed, and so are our genetic makeups. The complexity of the human genetic code is such a miraculous design that it has turned atheists into believers. Our DNA, when assigned notes, plays music so beautiful that Beethoven and Bach would stand to applaud.

Scientists now know for a fact that there are chemical differences between those who exhibit contrasting temperament types, and some have proved it by predicting temperament based on the delicate relationships of neurotransmitters such as norepinephrine, serotonin, dopamine, and histamine. Perhaps one day blood tests will be more accurate than personality profiles! Physical design plays into and affects one's soul as well. If our bodies, which turn to dust after just a few years, are designed with such care, how can we doubt that our eternal souls were made with the full creative force of our Creator?

In Psalm 139, David sings about both body and soul. His bones and woven flesh are not the only things God made marvelously well. God also paid attention to his thoughts, words, and will—the three things animals don't have, the elements that make a human soul. He ends with the reason for God's attention to these details: that He has David's life planned out. God has done the same for us.

> You know exactly how I was made, bit by bit,
> how I was sculpted from nothing into something.
> Like an open book, you watched me grow from
> conception to birth;
> all the stages of my life were spread out before you,
> The days of my life all prepared
> before I'd even lived one day. (vv. 15–16)

In the first chapter of his letter to the Ephesians, Paul talks in language reflective of two life arenas: architecture and family. Before God laid the earth's foundations, He had blueprints mapped out.

He took great joy in all this planning because He had glory to reveal and wanted to do it through mere people like you and me. And He wanted to reveal it in the context of family: Father and beloved Son; Father and countless adopted children. His plans included a strategy for our wholeness and holiness. He would make us by design, save us though the death of His Son, and give us an identity in Christ, which would come to its full meaning in a family.

> It's in Christ that we find out who we are and what we are living for. Long before we first heard of Christ and got our hopes up, he had his eye on us, had designs on us for glorious living, part of the overall purpose he is working out in everything and everyone.
>
> It's in Christ that you, once you heard the truth and believed it (this Message of your salvation), found yourselves home free—signed, sealed, and delivered by the Holy Spirit. This signet from God is the first installment on what's coming, a reminder that we'll get everything God has planned for us, a praising and glorious life. (Eph. 1:11–14)

Each of us is made to praise God and to bring Him glory. Our diverse temperaments sing different songs to Him. Our lives—and our mothering styles—show different aspects of His glory. What needs to be worked out of us is effectively worked out by the dynamics and challenges of family life and by the work of God's Spirit.

I can't be like you; you can't be like me. Nor should we try to be. We must embrace our temperament along with every other gift God has given us and invite Christ to use it all toward a "praising and glorious life."

How Deep-Rooted Is Temperament?

Temperament is not something we can really measure. It is a subset of personality. We see that someone easily talks to complete strangers with spontaneity and warmth. This is a personality trait. From this we can make the assumption that the person is extroverted and people oriented. Such a mom will enjoy talking to her kids, show affection, and give sincere compliments with ease. Due to stress, illness, or circumstance, her behavior could, however, vary greatly, but her *natural* tendency, her temperament, is likely to remain warm and outgoing. Her personality is the tree above ground, which will change shape and color from season to season, but the root system will stay the same, growing deeper as the tree matures. This invisible root system is temperament.

If temperament were ignored and exactly the same behavior were expected of all mothers, each could find a way to produce the required "fruit." Let's take as an example helping a high school student with math homework. A Boxwood mom (we'll get to know her later) would probably go to great lengths to study the curriculum so that she could assist her child every step of the way. The Pine Tree mom (she's going to be many people's favorite) would likely ask her Facebook friends for sites with free tutorials and would give her child the links for self-study. The Rose Bush mom (not too keen to make this her problem) would perhaps pay for a tutor's help, while a Palm Tree mom (not usually a homework lover) might suggest a study group with gifted students. Each mother's help would benefit her child.

Behavior is flexible. We can be taught—by our cultural environment, people, and the influence of the Holy Spirit—to act against our temperament in order to conform to expectations. We can learn to deal with our predispositions (for example, the tendency to ignore math completely), but the predispositions will not disappear. We can conform, but we will experience burnout as a result.

Severe trauma can change our fundamental being, and even then the true nature of our temperament will still sometimes break through the surface of our adopted personality. In unguarded moments, we will revert to our own deepest roots. When we receive healing for these hurts, we become ourselves again, not a strange new person. I often see people assessed with the same temperament results before and after deep healing. Different characteristics might have been dominant before, often many of the negatives. But after the restoration God brings, the beauty of this same temperament breaks through. You are still you, only whole and redeemed.

I can imagine that a free-spirited mother who suddenly has triplets on her hands would become structured and fond of lists as a survival mechanism. However, she would never have the sheer joy that the natural list maker has when looking at a grocery list that is color coded, neatly typed, and organized according to her local store's aisles. What is functional for a mom who has *learned* to act a certain way is foundational to the mom who *naturally* acts this way.

Many of us reject the idea of personality types because we always "test in the middle." This is because we have mixed temperaments. Perhaps one side shows at work and the other at home or among friends. This does not mean we have split personalities; we just have broader designs for broader purposes. Our personalities are underpinned by more diverse natural traits. This may make our behavior a bit harder to predict. Many temperament or personality models shy away from the difficult task of describing the unique patterns that emerge from a more complicated combination of temperament types.

What Will My Tall Trees Parenting Profile Tell Me?

The Tall Trees Parenting Profile (T^2P^2), which reveals the mothering styles we are about to explore, is able to integrate these complexities and make them understandable in practical terms even when you "have a little bit of everything."

Personality profiling tools are used these days for everything from team building to marriage enrichment to psychiatric evaluations and employment placement. The usual aim is to diagnose, direct, and determine. By comparison, the T^2P^2 puts the emphasis on relationship and aims to embrace, explore, explain, and expand. If a profile can lead us to understanding and loving acceptance of the diversity God has put into us, it is accurate enough.

The T^2P^2 is based on the many fourfold personality theories found in literature, studies of personality, behavioral and learning styles, and observations of parenting practice. At the heart of the T^2P^2 are four tree types: Palm Tree, Rose Bush, Pine Tree, and

Boxwood Tree (sometimes called a lollipop tree, topiary, or ornamental tree).

Palm Trees are jovial individuals with a love for people and the exciting opportunities life offers. Usually talkative and optimistic, they are the friends who keep the party going and help us stay mindful of the bright side of life.

Rose Bushes are born pioneers who tend to lead the way *their* way. Fast and determined, they ensure that nobody stagnates. Their roses are proof of their productive drive, while their thorns represent their tendency to be painfully honest.

Pine Trees balance out these extroverted tree types by being all about peace and harmony. They are content to let others lead and take the risks. They will provide the safe places and listening ears.

Boxwood Trees are the quality controllers. They believe there is one right way to everything and they strive to follow it. While the Palm Trees and Roses enjoy challenges and the unknown, Boxwoods prefer advance notice and only well-planned changes.

Trees were chosen for the test because they represent life, growth, potential, and beauty. No two trees are the same, not even trees of the same species.

Nobody fits perfectly into one temperament group. Most people have characteristics in two of the groups. Those who have traits in three groups are rare and gifted. In the T^2P^2, combinations of any two or three types render unique reports.

If you haven't already completed this assessment, I urge you to pause and do so now. See the preface for more information. After getting your result, look for the chapter in this book about your tree type. Are you a combination? If you're a Pine-Palm, read the chapters about the Palm Tree mom and the Pine Tree mom as well as the special section about Pine-Palm moms in chapter 8, "The (un)Natural Moms from Elsewhere."

Why Does Temperament Matter?

Many of us have allowed experiences, spouses, and even our children to distort who we are. Parents don't mean to, but they often have a preference for a specific type of child. Society certainly does, and so do some communities of believers. We are intentionally or covertly molded by our families and environments to have those ten or twenty most desirable traits. Many of us take to this molding, but many don't. Those of us who seek harmony resignedly follow the flow, while those who don't conform resist the assault on their individuality and defend their right to be unique within the boundaries of God's Word.

Any personality can love God with her whole being. Any personality can love her neighbor as herself. Such diversity adds color to our churches, marriages, and world. I believe it even adds color to heaven. You can probably say quite easily which of your godly role models loves God with heart more than with head, and who loves Him with strength rather than with emotions. We should not tamper with the beauty of these differences.

It is possible to stick pretty much any plastic fruit onto a tree. I've read that one can now even purchase fruit salad trees in Australia. Some bear as many as six different fruits! The grafting of multiple species into one tree does not change the species of the fruit any more than strapping a saddle onto a moose could turn it into a racehorse. It is never an apple tree that bears lemons.

But people often try to change one another's temperaments. The attempt to replace the natural traits in a person with more "desirable" traits is not only disrespectful but also harmful. Temperament points to our God-given calling in much the same way a compass needle points to magnetic north. If you can remember the science experiment from your school days, you will recall how aimlessly a demagnetized needle spins around its axis. It has lost its sense of direction. It was demagnetized by being rubbed with a magnet stronger than the magnetic properties of the needle. Strong personalities, dominant parents, hurtful messages, and punitive discipline can all act as demagnetizers. We too can forget where we're going in life. Some of us are so damaged we can't even answer the simple question "Where would you *want* to go?"

I meet many moms who have been bullied by models of motherhood that are simply as foreign to them as a saddle to a moose. They are no longer able to find their way to fulfilling motherhood. This often happens to a woman who marries into a different culture or marries a man with a strong opposite temperament. It also happens when leaders try to make clones of their followers. Trying to fit the mold becomes so exhausting to these moms that even their natural strengths wilt. They are the apple trees forced to bear pears and now bearing neither. Some of them are so cut up by legalism or rigid systems that they look more like bonsai than their natural selves. Once these mothers are given permission to obey the magnetic pull God created them with, however, they start blooming again.

The fundamental problem, I believe, is that we think the perfect tree exists. My "perfect" trees are oak trees. I like the shape, the bark, the leaves, the solid shade in summer, the hues of brown in the fall, and the smell of the soil in which they flourish. Are all other trees wrong or inferior? The spiritual teacher Ram Dass captured this well:

> When you go out into the woods and you look at trees, you see all these different trees. And some of them are bent, and some of them are straight, and some of them are evergreens, and some of them are whatever. And you look at the tree and you allow it. You appreciate it. You see why it is the way it is. You sort of understand that it didn't get enough light, and so it turned that way. And you don't get all emotional about it. You just allow it. You appreciate the tree.
>
> The minute you get near humans, you lose all that. And you are constantly saying "You're too *this*, or I'm too *this*." That judging mind comes in. And so I practice turning people into trees.[1]

Mothers are made to feel like the wrong tree. Can we counteract this by simply reciting the mantras "Live and let live" and "Be yourself"? No, that is not nearly enough. The idea is to know and be known, to understand and be understood, to appreciate and be appreciated, and to mature into what we are meant to be, all for the sake of whole relationships and a happy faith community that bears a large variety of fruit.

What If a Temperament Seems Ungodly?

Some say of temperament types that, like the animals in George Orwell's novella, *Animal Farm*, "all are equal, but some are more equal than others."[2] I disagree. When it comes to fulfilling our purposes in life and the Lord's purposes in this world, is there an ideal occupation, calling, spiritual gift, or place in the body of Christ? No. If all these aspects of creative design are varied and valued, there need not be an ideal temperament, either.

Similarly, someone who has an equal number of characteristics from each temperament type isn't necessarily more mature or spiritually balanced than someone with only one pronounced type. This more complex person simply has a broader design for a broader (not better or more ideal) life mission. Sanctification through the Holy Spirit is not the same as equalization; it is the process of setting us apart for a special journey. We will each still be unique. Spiritual maturity is not conformation to an ideal but rather transformation into the image of Christ. This image cannot be mirrored fully in any human individual. Christ is seen in only the collective mirror of all the members of His body—all of us bonded together by a love that does not compare, discriminate, or allow some to be superior to others (Col. 3:11).

Of course the temperament of Jesus included every good trait there was, but it suited His calling. He needed to be everything to every human being and carry every sinful tendency of every personality type in His flesh so that He could overcome all of it for all of us. Therefore, you and I need not aspire to be well rounded when it comes to a personality profile.

Still, there is never any reason for a mother, or anyone else, to excuse harmful or selfish behavior by playing the temperament card. Temperament is not a free pass, nor is it a box. Temperament is a gift that carries wonderful potential and distinct responsibility. Those who can must. Once you have found the beauty of your natural mothering makeup, you will know what you must do—must because you have the gift that others don't, must because others will suffer unless you live to the full, must because God intends to use all of you for His glory.

Insight into my own temperament tells me what I should be naturally good at; it also reveals what parenting mistakes I'm likely to make. Am I likely to be overprotective or uninvolved? Am I explosive to the point that I need to protect my children from myself sometimes? Am I so tolerant of their misbehavior that I need a "bad cop" to help balance me? As we look at mothers of every temperament type in the chapters that follow, we will see these parenting pitfalls. We may feel offended to be compared to these (un)Natural Moms when they act as we hope we never will. Their stories will not be identical to ours, yet they may hold valuable counsel to stay close to Christ, who makes us supernaturally natural so that the best of us comes out in our parenting.

Awareness of temperament can even help us be on the alert for our own potential moral failures, such as infidelity, intolerance, child abuse, addiction, and neglect. We can use these predictors wisely to be alert and sober minded, knowing that our enemy, the Devil, is always prowling around for prey (1 Pet. 5:8). Christ knows our weaknesses (Heb. 4:15); shouldn't we know them too? These weaknesses, needs, and character flaws tend to tyrannize us and make our lives tough. We have a choice: let them lead us into traps, or turn to Christ to help us overcome them. Temperament type, therefore, is not a predictor of godliness. The ways in which we express and indulge it or cooperate with God to shape it determine whether we will be more and more like Jesus.

God gives us a call, a vision and a dream by His Holy Spirit, a map in the form of a conscience, and a compass in the form of our temperaments. A fulfilling motherhood journey is somewhere close to our unique magnetic north, and by God's sovereign grace that journey can't be copied and pasted from a book or someone else's life.

For Reflection

1. How did the results of your Tall Trees Parenting Profile make you feel (surprised, affirmed, anxious, relieved, disappointed, hopeful)?

2. How do you tend to view your temperament? Is it a gift from God, a problem that needs correcting, or maybe something in between?

3. Have you ever parented in a way that is contrary to your temperament? If so, why? What was the result?

4. In what ways do you feel as if you are "not enough" as a mom? Where do you think these beliefs come from?

5. Which parts of your temperament are beautiful? How do your unique qualities bring glory to God and love to your family?

4

The (un)Natural Mom
on Boxwood Boulevard

Nurseries use the term *boxwood* for the ideal topiary tree. They are stylish trees often pruned into ornate shapes and used as decoration, especially in formal gardens. These trees appear tidy and controlled. When left unpruned, they form neat, round shrubs. The temperament type they represent is just as exemplary. Boxwood Tree moms desire to add style, sophistication, improvements, and the finishing touch that speaks of high standards. They love excellence. Boxwood moms seem almost perfect to people with other temperaments.

Boxwood shrubs are sometimes pruned into perfectly angular hedges and used as borders around yards or flower beds. Similarly, human Boxwoods love setting up boundaries between "this side" and "that side" of an issue. They want the lines drawn clearly. They seem to have an inborn sense of right and wrong. They comply to authority willingly and want others to comply too.

Interestingly, the thin trunks of boxwood trees are used for making finely crafted chess pieces and the tailpieces and tuning pegs of stringed instruments. People with Boxwood traits normally try to play by the rules of all games and of life. They can, like a boxwood in a pot, easily thrive in situations with strict rules and regulations. They definitely can embrace the idea that they are fine-tuners too! Like tuning pegs, they are eager to make adjustments toward perfection.

The wood is as moldable and dense as plastic but soft under a sharp tool. Boxwood moms can seem polished and shiny as well but are easily hurt. It is easy to shape them in the way one wants, which makes a Boxwood mom the likeliest mom to be "bent out of shape" by the opinions of others. She is the mom who will feel guilty when something not healthful is pointed out in her shopping cart. She will be embarrassed to have leaves out of place, so to speak. She'll try to adapt and may end up lost and demagnetized.

As we get to know our Boxwood moms better, we will often see them following chess-like strategies. They make their moves carefully. They anticipate problems and next steps. They want to be told how a mom should be and what she should do to make the cut. They are the most likely to read this book from cover to cover because of their hunger for learning. I hope they will read to the end, as they are the moms who may need the liberating news the most.

A Boxwood mom shares many characteristics with the personality type C (compliant, cautious, conscientious) featured in the DiSC model. She is called a melancholy by some. How liberating to know that she is so much more than that and need never be a victim of such a label. If you are familiar with these profiles, you may want to compare those insights with what you will learn in the next section about Boxwood moms.

A Day in the Life of Leanne

Before we get to know her, I want to put in a word for Leanne and every other Boxwood mom: here, as in the other profiles, my goal is not to describe a Boxwood in general but rather to visit one specific (un)Natural Boxwood mom, recognize her struggles, and offer grace to her and other moms like her.

Leanne is fairly raw as a woman and a mother. Unlike many of us, she had little in the way of a godly example. She is new in her walk with God and still indulges a number of her weak points. Perhaps that is why many of us whose T^2P^2 says we are Boxwood moms will resent being compared to her. We will be annoyed that she is a little like us and embarrassed that "one of us" behaves as she does. Some of us may even want to retake our profile because we don't want to be like her.

Remember that the Holy Spirit has yet to do a great deal of work in Leanne. And He will. She will still be a Boxwood, though! If we identify with her here and there, it is because we have some Boxwood traits in common, not because we are as far from emotional freedom as she is. None of us will be exactly like her.

Leanne is in her forties, married to Steven, a patient and poised Pine Tree. They have three children: fifteen-year-old Samantha, ten-year-old Doug, and seven-year-old Benjamin.

6:05 a.m. *In bed* The alarm rings but she is already awake. It was set for 5:25 as a warning. She likes warnings. She's been getting up earlier since doing the online course *Make Over Your Mornings*, by Crystal Paine. By getting important tasks done before everyone else gets up, she feels more in control. If she doesn't do that, she feels as if she's playing catch-up all day. She uses five minutes to go over the day's must-do list.

She breaks a little sweat as she remembers that Doug was supposed to have his permission slip completed and signed today or he will miss his science field trip. *The slip!* She has no idea where it is. She did not factor in five extra minutes to look for it, so she will have to fly.

She has breakfast and snack packs done by the time the children wake one by one. She finds the slip on the counter; there was really no need to stress. She takes Steven his coffee in bed and sadly wonders if she'll ever be on the receiving end of this treat. She sits with him for a few minutes—the hardest part of her morning but a worthwhile, intentional investment in their relationship. He gives her a long hug. She reprimands herself for feeling held up by it. He wants her to watch a funny video on his phone. She can't possibly fit that in as well.

7:05 a.m. *In the car* The past hour was not pretty. None of her three children was born with her Boxwood genes. They have alarm clocks. These mean nothing. The kids know what to do in the mornings. This too means nothing. She inevitably turns into a cuckoo clock, announcing the next task every five minutes: "Eat faster! Brush your teeth! Schoolbags! Lunch packs! Hockey sticks! In the car!"

As they pull out of the driveway, Leanne assesses ears, noses, hair, and armpits for undesirable sights and smells. Then she moves on to the daily Doom Report: "Benjamin, you could fail today's test. I told you nicely to study in advance, but I don't think you started early enough. I worry for you." When Benjamin doesn't show the desired amount of fear and remorse, she continues: "Go on like this and you will spend next year in Bully Bill's class. Is that what you want?" An oppressive cloud hangs in the car like stale cigar smoke. Life is serious.

The cuckoo clock has one last announcement: "Don't lose your new shoes." Leanne feels a little proud of herself today. She held back on her Boxwoodness. Usually she fires off the warnings in threes. She bit her tongue on "Don't forget to hand in the signed slip" and "Don't eat just the candy in your lunch pack" and "Be nice to the new kids!"

7:45 a.m. *At the office* She's in first. It gives her time to start the coffee the way she likes it and get ready for her day.

8:00 a.m. *At the office* She notices a text message that came in earlier from her Palm Tree friend Jessica, who wants to move their 10:45 a.m. appointment to 11:15. This is a disaster. Today's plans are balanced precariously with no room for last-minute changes. The day is over before it has begun. To her surprise she can accommodate Jessica and get things put back into something that could be called order, but Jessica should have been able to alert her last night. People just don't plan! On top of that, Jessica wants Leanne to notify Megan of the change. Megan is *Jessica's* boss! It's unfair to everyone, but Leanne forwards the text to Megan.

8:45 a.m. *In the boardroom for a meeting* Her phone rings. She excuses herself to take the call in the corner of the room. It is the school. Samantha has left her art portfolio at home. The selection of artwork for the expo happens today at twelve. Can Leanne please bring it? Leanne's body immediately pumps enough adrenaline for her to leap over an eight-foot wall. Her head spins while recalculating and reshuffling not only today's list but also tomorrow's. Having trained herself to look for the silver lining, she's able to find it. If Jessica hadn't moved the appointment, Leanne would not have the thirty-minute opening to come to her daughter's aid. The meeting continues and she makes careful notes while editing the sharp bits out of the speech she's going to give her daughter later today.

9:30 a.m. *Back in her office* She's still upset but now with herself. It's probably her fault that Samantha is such a space cadet. Certainly if she could have taught Samantha more responsibility and mindfulness, this never would have happened.

10:30 a.m. *Near the school* Leanne realizes that she would probably make a scene if she were to give the speech and portfolio to her daughter in person. Giving just the portfolio to the office lady, Penny, would be wiser.

Blushing with shame, Leanne knocks on the office counter. Gentle Penny gives her one look and comes around from behind the glass window, pulls up a chair, and puts a comforting hand on Leanne's shoulder. This gentleness is just too much. Too wonderful. Normally nobody wants to "hear all about it." Ever. Penny does, so Leanne starts eleven years into the past when her arty, sweet daughter drew her first picture of a pine tree but left it by the preschool's swings.

11:15 a.m. *Back at the office boardroom* Leanne makes her appointment with Jessica with seconds to spare. Jessica's boss, Megan, has proposed a completely unrealistic project with a much too short timeline and inadequate budget. Jessica is her optimistic self and firmly believes that Megan will succeed. Leanne will have to put everything in carefully researched terms to prove them both wrong. Her job is on the line if this project goes off the rails. She hears herself going into an emotional downward spiral and does her best to stay afloat. She knows to pray when this happens. She knows that God, not this job, is her source. She feels better for a while.

The day seems unproductive. Only three hours ten minutes left in her workday. So many items not yet ticked off as done. Nothing is ever done. That is what she finds equally exasperating about work and motherhood.

She needs to consult with a few colleagues about the budget, but her colleagues' criticism stings fiercely.

Even if they don't say it out loud, she can tell by their nonverbal signals that they expect more of her. She wants to tell them all to remember she can only manage the money; she can't fix the economy! In spite of what she feels, she manages to give everyone a polite answer.

A sharp headache is building up behind her left eye.

1:00 p.m. *In the break room* Leanne helps herself to coffee. The topic discussed in loud voices behind her is how much spending money is good for children. She returns to give them the name of a helpful online resource, but they seem more interested in disagreeing with one another than in reading what the experts say.

3:00 p.m. *At the school gate* Samantha doesn't look nearly grateful enough as she flops onto the backseat. Leanne can't help herself: "So, do I get a thank-you for wrecking my whole day to bring you your portfolio?" Without even looking up from the page of her latest read, Samantha lazily replies, "Oh yeah. Thanks, Mom, but it turns out so many kids forgot to bring theirs to school that Mrs. Cunningham gave us till Friday to get all of our stuff together." Leanne drives in icy silence for a minute or two. "Get your 'stuff' together? We should bring Mrs. Cunningham home to your bedroom, especially your closet. Then she can show you how to get your 'stuff' together there. This was the last time I cancel my 'stuff' to bring you your 'stuff.'" She instantly feels flushed with remorse but can't apologize just yet. This day is worse than most, and she really tries to handle stress in a way that harms no one.

3:30 p.m. *At home* "Grab your shoes, guys! Bags at the door, please! No TV until all your homework is done, okay? And tennis is at five!" She sighs a grateful sigh. Her home has order and structure, and the effort she has put in to achieve this was worth it. She rewards herself with a trip to the coffee machine with her favorite magazine in one hand. She's beyond feeling guilty about it. She did the research. Moms who take their edge off by drinking something are better moms. She also knows that French-press coffee has the most caffeine, filtered coffee has the second most, and her espresso machine, although a little pricey, delivers the best taste with the lowest amount of harmful acids and caffeine.

She checks the children's homework as they dutifully bring it for inspection. She helps them correct the mistakes and makes them put it in their bags before they're allowed to have a bit of free time. She returns emails, makes a shopping list, and sends Megan a birthday wish a day early, just in case. "Tennis time!" she calls into the basement. Three pairs of obedient feet can be heard almost instantly. The kids aren't perfect, but their tennis shoes are in the labeled box she made for each, and they all stick to the screen-time rules that are posted next to the TV. She has regained perspective on

Samantha's slipup. The child has a good heart. All her kids try hard. She's content for the first time today.

5:10 p.m. *In the car after dropping off Samantha and Doug at tennis club* Benjamin picks this moment to pop one of "those" questions:

"Do you use condoms, Mom?"

Leanne manages to keep the car on the road. She irons out most of the wild vibrato in her voice as she responds with phrases learned from the parenting talk she tunes in to on the way to work each morning: "I'm always here to answer any and all questions you have, Benji. You know that, right?" She wishes they were at home and she had time to gather her thoughts first, but she heard that these chats are best done in the moment.

"Uh-huh."

"Well, let's start with what you already know about condoms, okay?"

"Well, Clive told me he found some in his parents' bedroom, so I just wondered ..."

"Do you know what they use them *for?*"

"No, Mom, I just know it's better to be safe than sorry. That's what Sean said when I asked him."

"Okay, remember that we agreed you would not ask Sean or Clive questions about important things in life? Remember we said Mom and Dad would answer those for you?"

"Yes. So are condoms important in life, Mom?"

"Yes, very. And I'm going to need a little time to think about how to answer this one."

"That important, huh?"

"Don't say 'huh.'"

"Sorry, Mom."

"Well, I want you to have information that helps you and doesn't confuse you. At age seven, you don't need to know everything about atoms, but they are so important that if we handle them wrong, they can blow up the whole world! Did you know that?"

"That's cool!"

"Yes, it is, but it's also dangerous! So here's what I think you should know. You know about seeds and eggs in people's bodies by now."

"Yes, Dad has eggs, and Mom has seeds. Or is it the other way around?"

"See, now, if the people who work with atom bombs get something like protons and neutrons (kind of like seeds and eggs) mixed up, boom goes us! Condoms keep seeds and eggs away from one another so that babies don't get made when they shouldn't get made. Bad timing with babies can sometimes be like bad timing with a bomb. Do you understand?"

"Like, do people explode?"

"Not really. But they do get hurt badly. In their hearts. They get sad and angry sometimes. And if they make a baby and they are not married, they or other people could get ashamed too. Sometimes that also means the baby never gets his daddy to live with him."

"I wouldn't like that."

"We are so happy you were made exactly when you were, at the right time, because that way we were ready for you. Not everyone has such a happy story."

"You like being ready, don't you, Mom?"

"I didn't realize you noticed!"

"Mom, so do you use condoms, then?"

"There are many ways to plan when to make a baby. We are keeping things safe right now because we are happy to have just you three."

"Safe so you won't be sorry?"

"Well, being blessed with a baby could never make us sorry! But safe, yes."

Leanne is relieved. She feels the conversation went well. She hopes she wasn't too serious or preachy.

6:00 p.m. *On the way home with all three kids in the car* "Samantha, honey, I was really mean earlier. I'm sorry." Leanne would have liked to apologize privately, but they have a house rule that public rudeness deserves a public apology. Samantha leans forward and rubs her mom's shoulder.

"How was today's practice, Doug? Did Coach finally pick the team for Saturday, or is he still making up his mind?"

Doug mumbles, "Mom, it was fine. I'm tired."

"Oh no, did you get left out again?" Leanne jumps to conclusions with more speed than an Olympic athlete. She happens to be right this time. She starts building the case carefully. "Coach may be bearing a grudge about the time when ..." Doug lets her vent a little. It's how she processes things. He waits for the last sentence. Leanne always ends on a positive note after getting the disappointment out of her system. "I'm sure you'll have another opportunity. They pick reserves, don't they?"

Samantha takes the opportunity to change the subject. "What's for dinner?" Leanne just missed the turnoff to the grocery store, where she was supposed to pick up mushrooms and fresh cream for tonight's chicken à la king dinner. She beats herself up quietly. *What else will go wrong today? I can't make something different now—it's too late. It's going to be so bland.* She finally answers Samantha: "Bland chicken. That's what we're having!"

6:25 p.m. *Back home* The kids avoid the kitchen, where she frantically starts working on the doomed dish while putting items back in their places all over the house. By creating order in the home, everything on her inside also gets tidied up. She talks herself into a better mood and intentionally chooses to enjoy the evening. She hums a song to herself that always picks up her mood but makes sure no one hears her. She was told many years ago that she can't carry a tune in a bucket. She still believes it.

6:45 p.m. *Dad arrives* Without a word, Steven walks in, sets down his briefcase, and walks lovingly up to Leanne, who is so engrossed in the cooking and humming that his arm slipping around her waist might as well be a python. She swings around, screams, and thrashes all at once. Steven tries to hug her to calm her down. She pushes him away. "When will you ever learn? I hate surprises and you know it!" She cries the tears that have been accumulating since this morning. Steven can't figure out why a badly timed hug has to lead to this. His third apology hits home and she lets him make it up to her by helping with the last touches to the dinner.

The family eats together at the table, the way Leanne has always insisted. Everyone gets a turn to give their high and low of the day, and she makes notes on the calendar when Samantha starts mentioning the art exhibition dates. March is so cluttered that Leanne will have to have her arm operation before then. Who will feed the pets, do the dishes, water the plants, cook, and clean while she's out of action? She makes a note to put in a request for leave well in advance and to teach the kids how to do the laundry at least.

7:30 p.m. *In the TV room* Leanne loves the series they're watching, but she can't help feeling they would have a healthier household culture without television. Steven dismisses her arguments about the benefits and she lets it be. He seems to really need this time to unwind. Still, she feels he could do it just as well with a book. She wishes she had time to read every now and then! She tells Doug not to slouch and Benjamin to keep his feet off the furniture, warns that the TV may be loud enough to bother the neighbors, and finally decides there are things to be done.

After half an hour of tidying up, she glances over at the rest of the family, wondering if they would ever get up if she did not tell them when it was bedtime. She would try it out one day but not tonight. Tomorrow is a school day, after all. At exactly the right time, she cuckoos, "Bedtime, guys." She visits each one for about fifteen minutes. Benji gets a story, Doug tells her about his day in two-word sentences, and Samantha gets a back rub, which she still enjoys as much as when she was little. Leanne loves this routine. It sets her mind at ease that she has given each child a fair and equal bit of attention.

She retreats into the therapy room, as Steven calls it, to work on the scrapbook of their holiday in Orlando. She selects papers that match perfectly, plans the quotes, tries various layouts, and then realizes that there are urgent things to do tomorrow. She doesn't want to start this at a time when she won't be able to finish it. She decides to put it aside until she has three or more uninterrupted hours of free time. She wakes Steven in front of the TV. She'll ask him once to come to bed, but she won't fight with him if he doesn't. She has learned that nagging avails nothing.

She sets her alarm clock and is asleep in five minutes.

Boxwood through the Seasons of Motherhood

When one asks Leanne questions about parenting, she has the correct answers because she reads and attends courses. It is hard for her to allow others access to what she really feels. These private delights and struggles are in her journal. This selection of entries, extracted from multiple volumes over the years, gives us a fair idea how she approached the various aspects of the parenting process and how she is preparing herself for motherhood into the future.

Deciding to Start a Family

January 5 Personal goal: marry sometime in the next two years. Work on your weaknesses before then. I never asked Mom about family planning ☺. I miss her. It's been two years. Will have to ask Dr. Brooks.

January 10 Had appointment today with Dr. Brooks. All looks good. So relieved. He said average time for healthy female to become pregnant = 6 months. Ideal number of years to settle into married life according to literature = 4 years. Make it 5 to be safe. I could be a mom in 8.25 years! 2 years (to find Mr. Right) plus 5 years (settling in), plus 6 months (trying) + 9 months (pregnancy) = scary thought!

Four and a half years later, July 3 Heading to the Rockies for the long weekend. Not too high into the mountains—just gorgeous foothills. Altitude is supposed to be a risk factor. I think we may succeed at making a

"Made on the Fourth of July" baby. No champagne this time. Sparkling cider instead. It's going to be superspecial. Steven thinks we should leave something to spontaneity, but I'm packing a thermometer to pinpoint ovulation. It will be my secret.

Pregnancy and Birth

July 9 I asked at the pharmacy and they said one can sometimes pick up a pregnancy as early as five days after conception! We followed my cycle chart carefully and we were relaxed and ready. I can just feel I'm pregnant.

July 12 We did it! Steven made me promise not to get too excited too soon or to start buying stuff until at least eight weeks. Cried so much today. Joy and hormones and missing Mom. Megan says Dr. Brooks is a nice man but lousy doctor. Asking around today to find a doc with tons of clinical experience and got the most recommendations for Dr. Chetty. But then I heard that he is quick to opt for C-sections. Going with the second choice, Dr. Moon.

September 2 Ultrasound felt like an exam I could fail. My heart was pounding. The baby's too! So cute. Doc says it's all the fudge I ate ☺. I couldn't help crying. Even Steven had a hard time hiding how overcome he was. Measurements perfect for eight weeks but gave due date as March 25 plus or minus 4 days. An 8-day window is huge.

September 20 Supposed to be the end of the first trimester. Tired of being tired. Hate not being able to accomplish the things set out for the day. Dragging myself through a swamp of sinking sand at work. Still having crazy nightmares every week or so. Tempted to look them up in that dream dictionary, but Pastor Williams says that's divination and could make my fears even worse. Read Psalm 139 instead. I know You are knitting our precious baby with Your own hands, Lord! Help me not to worry so much!

November 1 Had 18-week ultrasound today. It's a girl! Samantha, after Mom. Made three lists:

1. Bought, made, and ready to go
2. Needs for baby room
3. Hospital bag checklist

Hoping Alice organizes the baby shower well in advance so I have time to buy whatever doesn't get picked.

Watched six birth videos. Made notes to take along on the day so Steven can remind me how to breathe. Picked the method where you can really control a lot of the worst pain. I'm not going to be a screamer.

February 25 Days are passing too slowly. I've packed and repacked the drawers of baby clothes again. Baby mustn't get much bigger. Still hoping for completely normal birth. Praying, praying so much.

May 10 Never expected things to go this way. I'm still unsure where God fits into this. I know He has never let me down, but it feels as if He did this time. Went into premature labor on March 5. Samantha started showing signs of stress, so Dr. Moon decided on an emergency cesarean with full anesthetics. I just cried.

When I woke up, Steven was there, holding Samantha. She was tiny and frail looking. He wanted to hand her to me, but I just wasn't ready. I slept almost all the time for three days. The nurses and Steven started her on formula. I was so angry. After three weeks, Dr. Moon diagnosed me with postpartum depression. I had to agree that I was really not okay.

Baby Days

June 3 Got breastfeeding going and am being weaned off antidepressants. Tried Gina Ford routine, but Samantha never drinks the second breast. Leaves me lopsided and then suddenly wants the other breast at nap time! I need structure that works. Never thought I'd miss work, but I do. Want to show something for my efforts at the end of a day.

July 19 Solved the feeding problems. Started scrapbooking again. Great outlet. As I collaged the prayers and blessings everyone sent when Sammie was born, my eye caught Romans 8:28. I think I've finally made my peace with God.

November 30 I know I said I wasn't coping. How could Steven have interpreted this to mean that I wanted his mom in my house? He may as well call me incompetent to my face!

March 5 Had fantastic first birthday party for Samantha. Worked so hard at it. Everything was Hello Kitty from the cake to her little party outfit. I hoped she would give her first step today, but everyone reminds me she's a preemie and may be a little late at everything. Shouldn't she have caught up by now?

Toddler Training

June 3 Seriously considering going back to work but can't imagine leaving Samantha with someone else full-time yet. Playschool three times per week may work. Feeling guilty. Glad I read about temper tantrums. Handled it right the first time she tried it. She hasn't tried again.

Four years later, January 2 Dougie is almost two now. Everyone told me things only get easier. They lied. Dougie seems to want to become his own little being over my dead body. Man, I miss my space! It's become unbearable to go to church with him. The other moms don't seem to care if their kids are noisy and disruptive. I think our church needs a parenting course for the young moms. Seriously. They are not doing well at laying the foundations for their kids.

June 7 Am following the advice for strong-willed children with Dougie. It seems to be paying off. He's definitely a bit better behaved than his cousins. Can't believe that my brother allows his three-year-old to go to bed so late and then wonders the next day why he fusses all morning.

We now have house rules that both Samantha and Dougie seem to grasp. I drew pictures for him and wrote the words for her. Before we bring out a new toy, I state the rules. The fights are much rarer now. I talk them through everything.

Finally completed the four-week meal plan to rotate for breakfasts, lunches, and dinners. No more decision fatigue! Now I know each day what to prepare. I think the kids will eat better now that there is more variety.

February 20 Can't believe we almost had another March baby! Benjamin is doing great. I don't think I'm strict enough with Dougie at the moment, but I just have to pick my battles. Can't fight them all. I pray I'm fighting the right ones!

School Years

March 20 Yesterday Samantha gave me a handwritten birthday card. She has learned so many skills. Helps me a lot with little Benji. I enjoy teaching her new things every day. Nice to be able to talk to the kids and have them talk back like intelligent beings.

School is working for us. I like the system. We know what to do every afternoon. Now that I'm back at work half day, it takes planning, but at least life feels more structured.

May 1 The homework is way too much. It takes me deep into the night to help Samantha with projects. I can't leave her to do it by herself or she'll never get any sleep. I've seen the other projects. The moms clearly help a lot, so if I don't, Samantha will get poor grades, even when she does her best. Can't the teachers see how unfair this is? I feel as though I'm cheating, but what option do I have?

I wonder if I'm too protective. I never let Samantha sleep over or go to a house where I don't know the parents and at least some of the kids. One can't be too careful, and I couldn't deal with it if I took a risk and exposed my kids to something harmful.

July 10 I saw a picture of a Chinese water carrier today and saw myself. Most things are a balancing act. A scorecard runs in the back of my mind at all times: How many sweets have they eaten? How many movies have they watched? How much time did they spend on chores? Are they getting fair chances at school? I know exactly how many times they've misbehaved. Am I mean?

Parenting Teens

March 5 Samantha turned twelve today. She's so sweet. I think we hit it lucky with her. No violent mood swings.

She still lets me manage most of her life, unlike some of the tweens I've seen. When other parents say, "You've grown up now, so you can decide for yourself," I envision Samantha on the edge of an abyss and me saying, "It's okay if you want to step over the edge." What are these parents doing?

Two years later, May 28 Fourteen is a scary age. Samantha doesn't tell me anything anymore. Makes me fear that she could get into dangerous stuff without my knowing. That book about praying for your kids just made it worse. It pointed out a bunch of hazards I never thought of. Yesterday's radio broadcast about kids and social media was the worst. Sexting? First time I heard of such a thing. Could Samantha and that Howard kid be doing that? I'm going to check her phone someday. If she catches me, will she *ever* trust me again?

One year later, April 12 I'm told I micromanage the kids too much. I have reason for fussing over the details. The devil is in there. Tried to give them more responsibility this weekend when we went camping. Let them pack their own bags. So, Samantha arrived without a beach towel and Doug packed no underwear (could have been on purpose). I don't think it's working for us.

One year later, July 7 Samantha is on a date and I'm freaking out right now. I know we raised her with good values, but I fear freedom of choice. I'll feel like a failure if even one of our children chooses a different path. How God deals with His children saying no to Him is beyond me.

Letting Go

September 1 Samantha's last year of school. Hope she picks a college close to home. My responsibility will never end, so why should I let go? I don't even allow sprinklers to run in the backyard without checking on them, so why would I allow my kids to run around the world unsupervised? We aren't even halfway through teaching the skill sets that I want the kids to have before they stand on their own two feet.

"Boxwood Gran" Years

October 10 Just heard Penny is going to be a grandmother! She hopes to be able to retire so she can take care of the baby for her daughter. I don't think I want to do that one day. I'll help out. I'll be an educational granny. I'll try to be less strict than I was with my own kids, but I'll have well-planned activities with paint and blocks and outings to interesting places. I'll be sure to treat all my grandchildren fairly.

I'll read up on the latest baby techniques so that I can come to Samantha's rescue whenever she feels a little overwhelmed. I'm going to make sure I have a ton of "baby hacks." She'll be impressed when I share what I've learned on YouTube, if it still exists then. Maybe I'll even have my own granny blog where I give tips to other grannies.

The Natural Boxwood Mom

Not all things in the mothering arena come naturally to dear Leanne and her fellow Boxwood moms. Still, they are moms who are intentional about every aspect of motherhood. The Boxwood parenting style is not popular just with bookkeepers like Leanne; even celebrities raising their children in the spotlight see value in the boundaries the Boxwood moms excel at:

> *Being in a position where they live such a privileged life, it is important that our children understand humility, that they appreciate how their parents have worked very hard to create this life for the family and that they, too, have a responsibility to work hard, be respectful and never, ever take anything for granted.*
>
> Victoria Beckham

> *[I aim for] consistency, and not making idle threats. They have to know there are consequences for violence, name calling, and not doing household chores. They're all in such different places, but all those places require boundaries.*
>
> Jennie Garth

> *Motherhood is the most completely humbling experience I've ever had. It puts you in your place, because it really forces you to address the issues that you claim to believe in—and if you can't stand up to those principles when you're raising a child, forget it.*
>
> Diane Keaton

*I'm strict about manners. I think that kids have a
horrible time with other people if they have bad
manners…. The one thing you've got to be prepared to
do as a parent is not to be liked from time to time.*

Emma Thompson

Let me turn the spotlight onto the things the Natural Boxwood
Mom is great at. When she focuses on the frustrations of parenting,
she tends to overlook these.

The Boxwood Mom and Nurturing

What the experts say: Leanne's hands-on mothering
style with lots of talking and interacting enhances brain
development and wires her kids for faster language learning.

Her love for routine creates a predictable environment
in which the relationship between cause and effect is
learned earlier, giving her kids an edge when it comes to
acquiring logical thinking and mastering mathematical
concepts. It even raises their IQ.

What her husband says: She hated having to let a baby
cry. Even when she had determined to stick to the carefully
researched sleep-training plan of some expert, she would
try to rationalize herself (and me) out of it: "They say it's
okay to let her cry for three minutes at a time, but what
if she's genuinely scared of something—a spider perhaps?
What if she has her little finger caught in a buttonhole,
or what if she can't roll over and feels anxious?" Before we

knew it, we'd both be back in the baby's room checking through twenty possible nighttime troubles. It turns out that experts now no longer advocate strict sleep training at such a young age. Leanne's instincts were right!

Leanne never misses a symptom or sign that something is wrong. She's really attentive. She often knows what's wrong long before the doctors do. She goes to them for medicine, not a diagnosis.

When we go out as a family, she is always armed with Band-Aids, fever medication, bug spray, an extra bottle, and a spare sleeper. It's because she knows where the greatest need is. I once found notes about the nearest hospital together with the printed packing list for our camping trip and brochures about educational outings in the area. It must have taken her hours to compile. I realized that this is clear proof of her love for us.

What her kids say: Mom always has a plan or schedule to help her take really good care of us. She makes sure we always have something really healthy and balanced to eat. We do get treats every now and then, but only if Dad hasn't yet spoiled us. She seems to have a calculator that tells her when we are behind or on par on some random vitamin.

What other moms say: She knows *everything* about children. When you're not sure, you call her. She'll give you a thorough explanation, and if you sound unsure she'll come over and check on you. It's like she's swallowed a medical journal, a pharmaceutical catalog, and the collective writings of a dozen pediatricians.

The Boxwood Mom and Discipline

What her kids say: Okay, this is where Mom is impossible to fool. She is supergood at sniffing out our mistakes, like a CSI agent. Don't think you can get into trouble at school without her finding out. Even if you've already been disciplined at school, Mom will take it upon herself to give you another consequence. She says she is the only one who will answer to God about our discipline, so she takes it seriously!

But she might let you get away with something the first time, especially if you cry a lot and show how sorry you are. And she is fair and doesn't punish us for accidents. She knows when we could have done better but didn't.

She has reward charts and other ways of keeping track of our behavior. We have figured out ways to get her to forget about those from time to time, but our distractions don't last long!

She learns her tricks from other parents and also reads lots of magazine articles about parenting. We guess it's hard to be a parent because we once heard her praying out loud for wisdom, saying, "Jesus, I don't know what I'm going to do!" Her prayers probably also help quite a bit.

She can't hide when she is angry or disappointed, even when she is on the phone and you can't see her face. It's in her voice. But she tries really hard to control it.

What other moms say: We don't know what she's fussing about. Her kids are perfect! We let things slide a bit during weekends or the holidays and even make exceptions when we just get tired of being the law, but she never slips up. She notices the little things about tone of voice, manners, disrespectful body language—everything. It is hard for her to let any of those things go unnoticed. Her kids have a great example in her for self-discipline.

What her husband says: She complains sometimes that I don't do enough of the disciplining in the house, but she's so good at it, I'm redundant! When things go wrong between her and the kids, she takes responsibility. She apologizes sincerely and with true remorse when she has hurt their feelings.

The Boxwood Mom and Training

What the other moms say: If your kids are in the same class, call her when your child's missed some schoolwork. She'll have the notes. She'll even know your child's schedule.

Her kids could say the names of all fifty US states before half our children could say, "Love you, Mommy." Her youngest knew the books of the Bible from Genesis to Revelation when he was four. She talks about good character—such as honesty, encouragement, support, service, and kindness—with her kids during their weekly family meeting. We don't even have family meetings. Those

101

things we always tell ourselves we should be doing as a family—she does those.

What her husband says: Leanne may forget that our kids will still have the capacity to learn after leaving our home, or perhaps she's just not sure that life will be a gentle enough teacher. She has printed out lists of skills she's determined for them to learn before they leave home. People actually download them from her blog! Still, I think if our kids managed to work their way through that list, she'd be anxious about them leaving anyway.

She has taught our kids an appreciation for beauty, creativity, culture, words, and music. There isn't a thing she won't do, a book she won't read, a course she won't attend if it promises to make her a better mom.

She has a natural knack for this. I just wish she could relax into it a little.

The Boxwood Mom Coping with Life in General

What the other moms say: We want to be like her. She can do it all, and what she can't do, she learns. Honestly, if she were skinny on top of that, we'd hate her. We think she's a nervous eater though. A better body is all I have on her. But even this was thanks to a diet she emailed me. She's an excellent source of trustworthy info.

What her children say: She is a great mom, and everyone but her can see it. She always acts thoughtfully. If we do something inappropriate, she makes us apologize. She writes notes, sends birthday cards, flowers, things like that.

What her husband says: Leanne is the manager of the household. I can trust her. She took over many of the tasks I had to manage before we got married. What a relief to know she has her hands on the details.

My dear Lee handles everything life throws at her but seldom seems to be coping. I had to learn that she is like a steam engine of the old days. She builds up pressure in order to keep going, and she lets out steam once in a while. The steam and the heat should not be interpreted as problems. She's not a car that should run cool at all times.

I've noticed how when I try to fix things for her or cool her down, it makes her even more upset. She works things out herself. It's as if I just have to put my arms and my love around everything she's feeling and saying, without judging her, until she settles down. I pretend to be a mirror and I just give back whatever she gives me. If she says it's the worst day of her life, I say, "Honey, you feel as if nothing worse than this has ever hit you." When I do this, it's almost as if she hears that she may have been a bit too dramatic. She might then say something like "I guess if this is my life's biggest disaster, I'm not the worst off, am I? I'm just so very, very upset!" Then I just do the same thing again and say, "You've seen people go through more horrific things than this, but this still is really bad." Three rounds of this, maybe four, and she calms down, thanks me for understanding, and makes a plan to solve her situation. I actually don't understand! But by not convincing her that she should feel better, she feels better. Go figure!

I've seen spiral-shaped boxwood trees in some fancy gardens. My Lee is definitely one of those. Her spiral just goes down instead of up sometimes. She tends to go down that dark spiral and lose hope for herself and us. She is about to go to a workshop for Boxwood women. It teaches them how not to become overwhelmed. I'm looking forward to seeing her implement these new principles. She can learn anything she puts her mind to.

She has a note on her bathroom mirror, which she both loves and hates. It reads, "Forgiveness is giving up on justice." She manages to forgive others but has a hard time forgiving herself.

My goal is to help her keep perspective. Apparently, the type of tree I am is good at that. We had some of our best family photos printed on a large canvas along with this quote by Pulitzer Prize–winning columnist Connie Schultz: "When you're in the thick of raising your kids, you tend to keep a running list of everything you think you're doing wrong. I recommend taking a lot of family pictures as evidence to the contrary."[1] We gave it to her a few years ago on Mother's Day.

Are You a Boxwood Mom?

Even if you share only a few characteristics with dear Leanne, you might be at home on Boxwood Boulevard, where dedicated moms love correct information. Here are some affirmations you may want to post somewhere for those days when you feel the urge to look for a more suitable mother for your children:

- I have made personal sacrifices of time, comfort, dreams, and luxury in order to raise my kids right.
- I am a natural at explaining, teaching, and giving detailed information.
- My children know how to handle structure, rules, and boundaries.
- I have given my children good examples of hard work and faithfulness.
- My kids and I are usually prepared, equipped, ready, and on time.
- I constantly learn in order to grow and improve as a mom.
- I take my duties as a mother seriously.

Perhaps you want your children, spouse, and friends to know that your Boxwood parenting style has its pros and cons and that you are willing to work on those aspects of parenting that don't come as naturally as others. Choose one or more of those challenges or any of the goals below to work on. Always choose these areas prayerfully.

Introspection can be dangerous because when we see only our mistakes, we might never look up again; if we look to Christ, He can remind us of the promise that He will finish the work that He has begun in us (Phil. 1:6). Safe introspection is done by following David's example. He opened his heart and asked God to look inside on his behalf and do the repairs that were needed:

> I feel put back together,
>> and I'm watching my step.
> GOD rewrote the text of my life
>> when I opened the book of my heart to his eyes.
>> (Ps. 18:23–24)

When we do this with the sincere desire to be more like Christ, God will lay a gentle finger on the things He wants to rewrite in our lives. If we could change ourselves, we would not have needed the cross. Jesus earned the power of change for us when He died without sin. He broke the tyranny of sin, which doomed us to keep wallowing in the mud. His power is called grace, and it is only by that grace that we can change. Ask Him where He would like to begin, and simply cooperate with a humble heart. Consider making commitments such as these:

- I'll use my planning skills to schedule rest periods so I don't burn out.
- I'll practice letting go and try to move on after disappointments.
- I'll set reminders to look for positives in each of my children and my spouse.
- I'll give people the benefit of the doubt when I'm unsure about their intentions.

- I'll watch my emotions and stop the downward thought spiral before it gets out of hand.
- I'll allow my fun-loving kids and spouse to drag me into enjoyable activities every now and then.

Are You Living with a Boxwood Mom?

Spouses and children of Boxwood moms sometimes feel as if they have to walk on eggshells. The thin skin and frail nerves brought on by a tough day like Leanne's don't make it easy. In exchange for all of her thoughtfulness, she deserves to be embraced as she is. Boxwood moms respond beautifully to the special fertilizer that suits them. The Boxwood mom in your life will find her own unique list in her Tall Trees Parenting Profile, but this general list of suggestions is a great place to start in helping a Boxwood mom be at her best.

These pointers will also help you see actions that make life difficult for her. Are you willing to take the first step to improving your relationship with the Boxwood mom in your life? If she knew that you sincerely wanted to help, she would say:

You can help me be more natural when
- You warn me of events or changes in your life so that I know you care that those changes will affect me, too.
- You try to understand that my feelings are not broken; the world is. Allow me to feel it at times and to cry about it until I can remember all the good things again. It may take a while.

- You don't tease me about my systems, routines, schedules, watches, or lists. I need to control what I can, and these are my tools of choice.
- You point out how well I do, when I do, and give me little notes of love and encouragement to show that you notice my efforts.
- You allow me to make it up to you when I have failed or hurt you. You might think it's best to just move on, but if I can't set things right, I can't move on.
- You remind me that things tend to work out, that God has never let me down, and that He assures us that this whole story ends well—we win! (But give it to me in writing because I might fight you on this if you say it at the wrong moment.)
- You speak gently to me, without harsh words or signs of irritation.
- You let me be alone when I look like I need to be. (Tip: when I'm becoming increasingly unpleasant, it's a sign!)
- You give me guidelines and information before you expect me to try something risky or new.
- You number the swords above my head in order of their importance to me. They seem like they're all going to drop at once. You can help me keep perspective.
- You patiently answer all the questions I need answered before I'm ready to give you a yes.

The Boxwood Mom's First Step to (super)Natural Motherhood

A Boxwood mom's high standards for parenting can create the impression that she has "arrived." This makes it hard for her children to reveal their own mistakes to her. Also, when she is tough on them for their own good, they may fail to experience the loving intention behind it and become resentful. When a Boxwood can admit this possibility, her children are likely to soften their hearts toward her.

I learned from a wise mother that a Boxwood mom often struggles to transition from mothering mode back into loving-wife mode when dealing with differences she has with her husband. Let us practice saying these words to our dear spouses and children, as our first step to (super)Natural Motherhood is admitting that we aren't perfect:

I am sorry that

- I tend to see what you're not yet doing well, all the while missing some of your best moments.
- I get worked up about untidy rooms and hair and other little things and miss the beauty of your heart.
- I forget there may be more than one good way to do something and that my way may sometimes not be the best either!
- I struggle to let go of tasks on my list in order to attend to your needs.
- I become emotional when we disagree and then tend to be irrational. Let's not speak when we're upset.

- I tend to wear my negative feelings like a banner and forget to tell you how much I love you and how proud I am to have you.
- I forget that you're an individual and that no book can give me a "recipe" for raising you (or being married to you). You can teach me many things.
- I am blind to my own mistakes while giving you a hard time about yours. You are allowed to tell me when I do that. Let's use the phrase "this is a plank and speck" when you feel I'm acting hypocritically (Matt. 7:3–5 NIV).
- I keep the child in me so deeply buried when you just need someone to have fun with. I will try to be playful and may need a little help from you.
- I expose you to my despair and feelings of worthlessness, which take over when I forget how God sees me.

Most of all, I am sorry that I sometimes doubt that you and I are God's gifts to each other.

A Boxwood Mom's Reflection of God's Heart

Leanne's love for **fairness** is a trait she shares with God. He loves fairness too. In striving for a world in which her children will be treated fairly, she shares the motive of our God, who constantly strives to lead us out of Egypt (a place of oppression and slavery) to the Promised Land (a place of peace, freedom, and a future). Leanne's name means "righteousness," and she strongly identifies with that.

She teaches a positive work ethic. She does this by not indulging or spoiling her children, always keeping them aware that there are no rights or privileges without **responsibility**. This too is a message God wants His children to understand. Every right we have by virtue of the price Christ paid for our sins is a gracious, undeserved privilege. It puts us in a position of stewards: princes and princesses appointed to rule wisely, not princes and princesses waited on hand and foot.

Leanne has a keen sense of **boundaries**, which is the foundation for all respect. She will not likely allow disrespect of any kind. Throughout the Word of God, we are taught that our love for God must be echoed in our love for people (1 John 4:7–12) and that this love is shown in how respectfully we honor God's image in every human being (Matt. 25:34–40). Do we respect their property, their marriages, their dignity, their contribution to the body of Christ? The entire second half of the Ten Commandments is about boundaries.

Leanne is the natural "law giver," much like Moses was. Though the Law could not make men holy (as Paul points out throughout the books of Romans, Hebrews, and Galatians), the Law did an important thing: it showed us our flaws and therefore our need for a Savior (Rom. 5:20). Leanne will likely play this role in her children's lives. She'll train their consciences. She won't leave them thinking they are always right and flawless. A conviction of their own mistakes will sometimes come out in her **correction**. Hopefully she will do it in a way that points them to Christ and not in a way that urges them to be better in their own strength.

Excellence characterizes everything Leanne does. God's entire creation has the same overtone. Details are as important to God as they are to her. When God gave instructions for the building of the ark, the tabernacle, and the temple, He did so in fine detail with exact numbers and measurements. Leanne tries to keep to the fine lines of God's expectations today.

God is a God of **order** and **discipline**. Leanne probably says this to her kids often! By growing up to value tidiness, punctuality, routine, and work in or around the house, her kids could find it much easier to serve God through humble, mundane, and invisible acts of servant leadership. Her faithful **service** to her family in housework and other duties sets the example. Discipline, to her, is providing that faithful service even when one doesn't feel like it. God can do much in the world with servants who do that.

Leanne is **thoughtful** and probably is training her children to be mindful of others. Her example of remembering birthdays, giving advance notice, and listening to the opinions of others in order to learn from them will hopefully rub off on her children so they can be the ones in their household, church, and circle of friends who build a culture of caring—the kind of caring that will let all people know we are Christ's followers (John 13:35).

For Reflection

1. What are your parenting boundaries? That is, what about being a good mom is nonnegotiable to you?

2. Which parts of Leanne's day resonated with your own experience? Did you resent being compared to her? If so, why do you think you felt that way?

3. How does feeling in control—of your schedule, of information, of outcomes—help you be a better mom? In what ways does your need for control work against you?

4. What do you feel is your greatest success as a mother?

5. Name one strategy you can put into practice the next time you are feeling overwhelmed by everything that you are doing "wrong."

5

The (un)Natural Mom
from Palm Beach

Imagine yourself in a convertible driving down Beach Road somewhere in California, Florida, or the south of France, wherever you
imagine the ideal beach vacation spot to be. Can you imagine it
without palm trees? People with this personality are the ones we can't
imagine celebrating life without. They usher in the sun and the fun.
My twin brother is such a jovial soul. We simply can't have family
celebrations without him. We have flown him in on occasion in the
same way resort developers import Florida palm trees to the heart of
Nevada.

Palm trees do not change significantly as they grow. The lower
fronds dry up and the trunks grow taller, but the waving treetops
stay the same. People with this temperament keep their childlikeness
too. They are grown-up kids who help us remember how to let our
hair down. Their sense of humor can sometimes leave us gasping for
breath. The children in them connect with the children they are raising
and can occasionally make Palms forget to be the adult in the house.

The coconuts these wonderful trees produce are known for their
variety of uses in high-fat/low-carb cooking, sweet-smelling tanning
oils (the ultimate fragrance of leisure), and rich skin-care products.
There are wax palms, sugar palms, wood palms, and açaí-berry

palms. Everything for a romantic weekend can be harvested from them, from the wax for scented candles and the vegetables for hearts-of-palm salad to luxurious bath oils, chocolate-covered dates, and Pindo palm wine. This makes a palm tree the perfect metaphor for the personality type that thrives on the sensual and exotic wonders of life and that strives to spoil others with special treats.

The Palm Tree temperament corresponds well with the sanguine temperament and also with the personality type I (influential, inspiring, interactive) of the DiSC profile. If you are familiar with these profiles, you can keep this in mind as you read on.

A Day in the Life of Jessica

We are about to meet a Palm Tree mom who might seem immature to some of us. Age plays a part in how our temperament is displayed. Jessica will become less whimsical and self-centered every year. Life will do that to her naturally. At this age, she is about as lively as she'll ever be. If you are an older Palm Tree, you'll likely recognize some of her characteristics as traits you once had but no longer display. You will wish she showed more depth of character, but you'll also feel sympathetic, knowing that others sometimes underestimate you as well. Perhaps you may miss your more carefree years, when your biggest problem was discovering that you forgot to paint your nails!

If your Tall Trees Parenting Profile gave you Palm Tree as a result, look for the traits in Jessica that others have pressured you to give up. Hold on to the beautiful ones or, if you have already let them go, work them back into who you are as a mom.

Jessica is thirty-five and with husband Randy, a steady Pine-Rose, has three young children: six-year-old Harry, dainty three-year-old

Vera, and two-year-old Nicola. Jessica works as the personal assistant to Leanne's colleague Megan, whom we'll get to know better in the Rose Bush Garden.

6:00 a.m. *In bed* Jessica wakes from a dream and wishes she could go back to it for just ten more minutes. The dream was so real that she could taste, hear, and feel every thrill. With a silly tune from a musical and words she makes up as she goes, she starts getting ready for the day. Life is good: she received the great news yesterday that she made it to the second round in the Mrs. Personality USA pageant!

Nicola toddles into the dressing room with her own makeup kit, imitating Jessica, who's making herself even prettier than usual. She interrupts her process to start coffee and switch on the pancake griddle. She runs back to curl her hair and hands over the preparation of the pancake batter to Randy by singsong-calling loudly from the bedroom, "Hon, be an angel and get the pancakes going, will you? I just need to finish here. The coffee will be ready in a minute!" Ten minutes later, she has not finished her hair but has pinned a few great recipe ideas to her Pinterest dessert board, liked the pictures on Facebook of the birthday party last weekend at her colleague's lake house, downloaded one shot in which she looked great, and made it her new profile picture. She loves how the dress complements her complexion and decides to wear it for round two of the pageant.

6:50 a.m. *Kids' room* She walks into the room Harry and Vera share and cuddles them out of their deep sleep. She kisses them both on their adorable chubby faces, whether they like it or not, and slings a sleepy Vera onto her back for a mock pony ride to the kitchen. She props her into her seat at the table, then runs back to find Harry not in the mood for his pony ride today. "I know why you don't want to ride this pony. What pony walks on his hind legs, right?" She promptly drops to all fours, shakes her hair like a horse's mane, and neighs like a proper horse. "Sir Lancelot, thine steed is ready to carry thee to thine delectable morning feast in the dining hall of thine palace." This does the trick, and soon everyone is at the table, enjoying a meal to the music of Jessica's incessant and excited monologue.

7:00 a.m. *In the kitchen* "So today is Mommy's big day. The newspaper people want to talk to Mommy about the competition. No, Nicola dear, don't throw the pancake on the floor. Here, let Mommy help. Hon, you'll remember to pick up the kids from school today? They can't say how long the interviews will take. Vera, sweetie, you have to eat now; it's almost time for school. They want to know everything about how I handle all of my tasks and motherhood and fitness … and no, I won't tell them that story about when you tried to do the triathlon with me, don't worry! They'll ask mostly about motherhood because I'm the only semifinalist with three young kids. Harry, why the long face? This is your favorite meal! Okay, hope you all had enough, because it's time to go!" Jessica gathers special clothes for the interview, diaper bag, bottles, a pacifier, favorite teddy, and all the necessary snacks by running around and up and down the stairs without getting out of breath. When they reach the car, they're only ten minutes behind the schedule Randy would like them on.

7:15 a.m. *In the car* In goes the kids' song CD. Those who can sing, sing along. Jessica sings the loudest, but her mind is elsewhere. Isn't her friend Denise flying to Thailand today? Without turning the music off, she calls Denise, who can do a quick coffee this morning around nine. That means Jessica won't make it to the meeting with Megan and Leanne. She keeps one eye on the road and one on her phone as she texts Leanne: "Something super important just came up. Won't make our 10:45. Can make 11:15. K? Pls tell Megan 2.☺xxx Jess." She decides not to look at the response. Leanne can be a little uptight sometimes. She's not going to let that spoil her day. She was going to take baby Nicola along to day care at her office as usual, but now dropping her off would be a half-hour detour. She makes a plan. She'll drop off all three kids at school quickly, have a great time with her friend, and be back for the meeting. It will be fine!

7:30 a.m. *At preschool and adjacent elementary school* Jessica hugs Harry and watches as he disappears through the gate of the elementary school. She holds Vera's hand and carries Nicola on her hip, avoiding eye contact with the two preschool teachers who saw what happened two years ago when she was late for the third day in a row to pick up Harry. The principal reprimanded her in front of everyone. Jessica never would have come back to this school if her husband hadn't insisted. She hates being hated. She gently nudges Vera into her classroom as they pass the door, hoping to stay out of sight.

She keeps right on going to the last class now, where the two-year-olds are. She prays there is a caregiver on duty who doesn't recognize her. It's her lucky day, as most days are. She smiles warmly and hurriedly explains, with touches of truth interspersed with fantasy and drenched in optimism, that a friend will miss a plane if she doesn't rush off immediately and that her other kids were raised here at this preschool with loving care, which gives her great confidence that she, the new caregiver, will be perfect to watch over Nicola for just a couple of hours until Jessica can collect her and take her to her usual day care at work. Without waiting for a response, she plops Nicola down next to a sedate-looking boy and gives her a toy and a kiss, thanks the stunned caregiver, and speeds out the door with, "They have all my details at the office, but there won't be a problem!"

9:00 a.m. *Across town at a restaurant* Jessica throws both arms around her friend, complimenting her hair color and apparent weight loss. "You look like a star,

Denise!" She doesn't notice that her friend has her eyebrows painted on with eyeliner and is awfully pale. She babbles about how she too lost a few pounds and just in time, seeing as the second round of Mrs. Personality USA kicks off in a week. Denise lets her talk and responds with the enthusiasm that has made her Jessica's favorite long-distance friend. When Jessica takes a breath and a sip of coffee, she notices that Denise is wearing a wig! A sea of realization washes over Jessica.

Jessica starts crying, "No, Denise, no! Please tell me this is a joke! No, please, Lord!" Her fears are confirmed by the tears that well up in Denise's eyes. Jessica leaves her chair, holds her friend tightly, and cries openly. "I can't lose you, Denise!" Just as suddenly as she choked, she dabs the tears from her cheeks and lights up with a broad smile. "Silly me. Of course you'll be fine. You're going to get better, aren't you?" In spite of Denise's wordless shrug and sad shake of the head, Jessica maintains the denial. "Denise, these days few cancers are fatal. I've heard amazing things about people coming back from the brink of death! Really! Have you tried the grape-seed diet and some alternative options? We can take you to the prophet with the healing ministry, what's his name?" Finally she runs out of ideas and Denise just smiles bravely.

"I'm here to say a final good-bye, Jess. I'm not flying back to Thailand. I want to spend the time I have left with my family in California. There's no more to be done for me."

"Of course! Your parents must be devastated. I'm so glad now that you never had kids or a husband who would have had to go on without you! It must be the hardest thing to lose a spouse. I couldn't raise my kids all by myself if Randy got sick and died. And if I got sick, they would never be okay."

"Stop, Jess. I just need you to accept this!"

Completely at a loss for words, all Jessica can string together is, "I'm so sorry! I'll try. I'm better with celebration speeches. I don't know what to say. Please tell me what I can do."

"Just enjoy this hour with me, that's all."

After a recap of their fondest memories, Jessica tearfully goes to her car. On the way, she glances at her phone and finds a message from Megan: "I don't appreciate your canceling a meeting by texting and having it forwarded by someone else. This will be the last time you disrespect me this way."

Jessica makes a face and a note to herself that Megan is having a bad day. She'll get Megan her favorite salad for lunch later. It should patch things up.

11:10 a.m. *In the boardroom* She prides herself in being early for the meeting with Megan and Leanne. She's proving that preschool principal wrong. *PRESCHOOL!* She forgot to pick Nicola up on the way to the office! No wonder she's early. She could call, but then they'll insist that she come immediately, which she can't do.

She feels they would have called by now if there were a real crisis. She doesn't even notice the missed-call notification.

Megan introduces a brilliant project. They can be done by March. Jessica proposes a few ideas for the launch and press release. Leanne has budget concerns as always, but Megan makes the final decision and dismisses the meeting.

12:45 p.m. *At the deli across from the office building,* Jessica asks for extra feta and olives in Megan's chicken salad. While it's being prepared, she pops in next door for Seattle's Best Coffee, Megan's favorite.

1:00 p.m. *In Megan's office* Megan tries not to show how pleased she is about the lunch, but Jessica knows her well enough. Jessica wants to tell her about Denise and why she just had to see her, but Megan is not in the mood, so she backs off. Megan is a great boss. She always makes it clear where one stands with her. Jessica doesn't take it personally. She would like more appreciation every now and then, but she gets it from the other senior partner. It's okay. She is paid well, and that can be taken to mean that her work is valued. She gets back to work. It's hard to focus because she's imagining the questions the interviewer might ask. She must remember to have her best side facing the camera. Her nails aren't painted! She'll have to make a plan.

3:00 p.m. *At her desk outside Megan's office* Megan storms out, slams down work files, and knocks Jessica's nail polish right out of her hand onto the teak desk, where it bleeds a pool of criminal crimson. Megan makes a strange request, which Jessica will never fathom but dutifully obeys: "Scan through my workload for files and mail that I can take care of at home. Have it ready by two thirty daily." As soon as Megan is out the door, Jessica cleans up the spill and grabs her things. She has her interview at four and still needs to change at a friend's house on the way. Nobody will miss her now that Megan is out for the day, so she can take the hour off. No harm done.

4:00 p.m. *In the lobby of the Holiday Inn* Photographers and journalists are already interviewing contestants in high heels, cocktail gowns, and sashes as Jessica walks in, wearing a tight-fitting plum dress and diamanté stilettos. She turns heads and pretends not to notice. She loves this. A representative drapes her Mrs. Personality USA Semifinalist sash over her shoulder and guides her to the corner where the interviewer awaits her. The interview takes more than an hour and she's asked twice to quiet down a little. The contestants around her find Jessica's laughter and loudness distracting. She wonders how they expect to be awarded a prize for personality if they can't even make themselves heard. She leaves at five thirty thoroughly energized.

6:00 p.m. *At home* Randy is glad to hand over the baton. It is animal hour and all three kids are exhibiting primal noises and needs. The moment their mom walks in, the cries escalate by ten decibels. Jessica tells the already exhausted Randy everything about the interview while tickling and piggybacking the kids into the big bathtub in the master bathroom. This is a special treat they usually have to earn with good behavior, but tonight is one of those "yes nights" on which Jessica would have agreed to ice cream for dinner. Randy wants to confront her for leaving Nicola at the preschool (for which he had to take the heat), but he can't get a word in. Jessica gets the kids dressed and makes a face when she discovers that Randy hasn't fed them yet. "Guess we can have Friday food on a Monday!" She grabs a few carrot sticks and some sliced fruit from the fridge for the kids to nibble on and makes toasted cheese sandwiches in a pan while still telling about her day.

7:30 p.m. *In the baby's room* Nicola is not herself because she should have been in bed by seven. Jessica tries singing, rocking, and "Three Little Kittens" to no avail. She knows that sleep is like a bus in a small town: it comes around every so many hours and if you miss it, you miss it. She gives Nicola a portable DVD player with her favorite cartoon to make up for the disrupted evening. *Routine* is a swear word in Jessica's world, but she knows the value of it in her children's world and prefers everyone to be in bed by eight at the latest. Nicola seems appeased for now.

8:00 p.m. *In Harry and Vera's room* Vera is already asleep and Harry is weepy, as he usually gets at bedtime. Too many things were out of the ordinary today. It rocked his boat. Jessica has a low-energy game in mind. She slides into bed next to him, holds him, lets him tell her all about his day, and starts teaching him how to speak Pig Latin until they laugh so hard they wake up Vera. By nine, all the kids are finally tucked in. She'll never get how other people just dump kids, switch off lights, and leave. This is the most fun time of her day!

9:15 p.m. *In the kitchen* Jessica pours glasses of champagne for her and Randy. It is, after all, a day worthy of grand celebration. She thanks Randy for handling the preschool and explains the crisis with Denise. She suddenly has a great idea. Does Randy think it can count toward her fund-raising initiative for Mrs. Personality USA if she did a cancer drive for Denise? Randy is in awe of the emotional extremes Jessica is able to accommodate and communicate. He knows she does this pageant to impact people. She has just turned tragedy into charity, after all.

10:00 p.m. *In bed* Jessica tickles Randy's ear and whispers something flattering. "Jess, you can't be serious! All I can think of is your dying friend Denise!" The night doesn't end as Jessica had hoped, but by tomorrow morning she'll be over it.

Palm Tree through the Seasons of Motherhood

Jessica's interview was titled "Mrs. Personality Contestant Is a Mother with Style." This is the Q&A published about Jessica three days later.

Deciding to Start a Family

Q: Did you always want to be a mother?

A: Yes, absolutely. I grew up with a clutter of cousins and Thanksgiving gatherings where we struggled to fit everyone into one picture. A large family was definitely one of my dreams since childhood. When I got married, the actual decision was a little harder to make. I knew having kids would mean the end of carefree life with my husband. I was scared of being tied down by bottles and nap times, for sure.

Q: How did you make the big decision?

A: We didn't really plan exactly when to start. We just felt ready after a few years.

Pregnancy and Birth

Q: So how did you respond when you found out you were pregnant, and did it differ with each of your three kids?

A: I love surprises, so, although I was a little shocked with the first one, I got excited within a few minutes and went shopping. Retail therapy works well to help you come to grips with the news. We told everyone at a family gathering two days later. (I would not have been able to wait longer. It felt like a month!) We suggested that everyone take a turn to make up a limerick about his or her family. My mom immediately started screaming with joy when she heard ours:

There once was a couple with pride
With a secret that they couldn't hide
A bump was fast growing
And with it the knowing
That they would soon hold a sweet child!

And I made a decision to enjoy every moment. I never gave up the things I love—even the things that made me gain quite a few pounds! Did you know that polar bear mothers have to gain around four hundred pounds? It's said that if they don't do enough midnight feasting, their bodies can reabsorb the fetus! I used this excuse when making myself sandwiches with Doritos and mayonnaise, topped off with microwave caramel brownies!

The second pregnancy was more planned because we had an overseas tour in mind and didn't think it would gel well with two babies in diapers. That explains the three-year gap. I decided to exercise more that time, wanting to gain a little less weight. The third baby, little Nicola, was a tougher decision. People had warned me that you cross the line from household to circus at this point. They were right. There has never been a dull moment since. But I firmly believe that all gifts from God are good!

Q: Mothers have such diverse birth experiences. Were the births the best moments of your life?

A: Without a doubt. Holding our babies for the first time and seeing myself and my husband imprinted in their features is a thrill I can't describe. I wanted my birth memories to be pleasant, so I opted for maximum pain relief from the beginning. I was lucky with the first two. I had spinal epidurals and my husband, mom, and two best friends were present. It was great. With the third, it was all drama, though. Nothing went as planned and I ended up having all sorts of procedures. I knew that we wouldn't be able to control these details, so I went with it and just held on to God. All that matters in the end is that the baby is healthy, right? And seeing as they had to do a C-section with Nicola, I opted for a mini tummy tuck that the doctor said he could do to make up for the drama. I felt I deserved it after putting my body through pregnancy after pregnancy!

Baby Days

Q: Did you enjoy the baby days?

A: Everything about your life changes in a heartbeat. It is exciting, but some losses are hard to accept at first. I missed my friends. My angel boy became my whole world. Some days I talked to my baby boy about how frustrated I was about my skin breakouts due to all the hormonal changes he put me through. I had no other company. Poor thing!

I breastfed for as long as I could and the pounds melted away, which was great. Once I could take Harry everywhere with me, I started loving motherhood. When I had Vera and Nicola so close together, I felt a little stuck again. Taking two babies in diapers and one four-year-old with me to visit a friend or go shopping was too much. It depressed me that I couldn't go to the gym or get my hair done when I needed to. It was just the inability to go out on impulse and especially to go out in the evenings that I missed. Babies require planning, which is not my favorite thing.

I think I would have gone barking mad if not for my friend Penny at church, who agreed to babysit for me once every two weeks so I could just go out for a few hours. Having my mom close by really helped too. She's a cool granny. After breaks from all the baby duties, when I got back I felt like cuddling those little bodies again. It did me a world of good.

I enjoyed my babies to bits—don't get me wrong! The freshly bathed–baby smell, the dress-up with my girls, the first tooth, first steps—I really celebrated all of that. They were and still are reminders of how God loves us. Can you imagine how boundless His love for us must be if it is infinitely deeper, wider, higher, and longer than our own love for our children?

Toddler Training

Q: Are you a strict mom?

A: I don't think so. I don't think it is necessary to be all serious. I always say happy kids are good kids. It's about making your home fun for them, keeping them busy with lots of activities that keep them out of trouble. You need to get down and dirty with your kids, take them places. We go on outings at least twice a month—somewhere the kids can run and climb. I let them make messes in the backyard too. You can't keep everything clean and orderly when they're this young. I'm convinced messy play is how kids learn.

I do have a few things that I am strict about, like the amount of sweets they eat. It's for their sake and mine. Hyperactivity runs in our genes, and one doesn't need to add sugar to that!

They have to know one thing: how crazy I am about them. I keep their artwork pinned up all over. I never want them to lose that childhood fearlessness and creativity! If they feel good about themselves, they will go through life a lot easier than kids who always fear punishment.

Q: Isn't routine important?

A: I don't make things too strict or hard around the house. I figured out ways to get two things done at the same time, like cutting hair and nails on the same day. You know those trays that fit over the edges of a bathtub? I sometimes use them for my two older kids to eat their dinner on during bath time.

I find that when kids misbehave, you just distract them to something more interesting, which strictly routine-bound people don't do. When the preschool teachers complained about my kids getting into trouble, I always asked if it happened during playtime. Usually it didn't, which proves my point that the kids just weren't having enough fun. Bored kids act out within restrictive routines.

I will admit that Harry, my oldest, seems to need more structure than comes naturally for me. I had to get more organized for his sake. My impulsive changes to our routine upset him too much. I had to give up a lot of that spontaneity so he could feel secure.

School Years

Q: How do you think the school years will be?

A: My oldest just started first grade. So far it's going well, but he is not like I was. He is the teacher's pet.

I want all my kids to participate in everything so that they can discover what they love. If they try out something for a while and decide it doesn't really float their boats, I will allow them to try something new. Some parents drag kids to soccer practice by the ears for a year just because they signed up once. I don't see the point in that. Here I am as proof that you can do what you love and succeed! That's all I'll ask of them in school: do your thing, be a good friend to everyone, learn teamwork, and don't be in such a hurry to figure out what you want to do with your life. Don't grow up before you need to.

I'll make our home a fun place to be. They'll have friends over all the time. I pretty much know all the kids their age and many of the parents already. I'll make sure we plug into activities in the community and build a good support system.

What's hard about school is all the paperwork and how everything revolves around an inflexible calendar. I was used to just tackling each day as it comes. Now I have to think three, four days in advance. It's exhausting! My playful side disappears altogether when I get all serious about the days of the week and what happens when. I become a whole different person that I don't even like.

Q: What about the academic side of schooling?

A: Schoolwork was tough for me growing up and really depressed me sometimes. Especially the bland book knowledge that you were supposed to memorize. Why couldn't we do something practical and physical? I think that is one of the reasons I was a rebellious teen. I just felt like the school was trying to squeeze me into a box. When my kids get that kind of homework, I'll help them get it done fast. The kind of person they become matters more to me than their grades.

Parenting Teens

Q: So you were the kind of teen some parents may have feared. What if your teen kids turn out to be trouble?

A: I'm a little nervous about that. My boy, Harry, is better behaved than I was. I was wilder, as I remember it. Sermons and curfews didn't change my behavior, so I don't plan to get after my kids too much even once they are teens. I read somewhere that if we give our children a taste for the things of God when they are little, the buffet of the world won't satisfy them. I'm going to raise them with the right values and within a group of good people, and hopefully they will come around even if they take a brief detour to establish their individuality, like I did.

Q: You sound like an optimist. What if your plans and prayers don't work out?

A: I think I'd be really mad if they did something illegal like drinking underage or driving without a license, but kids will be kids, won't they? You can't really control all they do. Sometimes it's even better not to know everything they get themselves into. I just want to be that friend to my teens one day, the person they come and talk to when they fall in love, when they get their heart broken, and when they mess up. I'm straight up about my mistakes, so I hope they will know they can be too.

Letting Go

Q: Your participation in this pageant involves doing something for yourself. Many parents may feel it's the time to be focusing on your kids instead. How do you strike a balance?

A: The secret is to never stop having fun and to continue through the mothering years with whatever keeps you cheerful. My mom is a lot like me. She took dance classes as a teen, did ballroom with my dad throughout my school years, and started belly-dancing classes in her forties. By her fifties she was excellent at it! I have a life that's bigger than just my husband and kids.

Q: Won't you regret this once they each head out on their own and leave you with an empty nest?

A: I've thought about those years when I'll have to let go. I really don't want them to leave. I think I need them to need me to make them happy, if that makes sense. If they find happiness somewhere without me, I might feel like I've failed them. So I think I'll keep on creating reasons for them to come over! As far as an empty nest goes, my nest is always teeming with pleasant people. There are many pleasurable things I will still do in my fifties and beyond, I'm sure of it.

"Palm Granny" Years

Q: What role do you think grandmothers play in kids' lives, and what kind of a granny do you plan to be?

A: I'm going to be the granny the grandkids adore and the in-laws despise! I will spoil the kids rotten. I'll feed them candy and treats. I'm going to do nothing that makes them cry. I hope I'll have enough money then to buy them scandalous birthday presents just to see the looks on everyone's faces. I'll stop if my kids get really upset, of course. But a granny is allowed to break the rules sometimes. My mom is like this, and my kids worship her.

The Natural Palm Tree Mom

Palm Tree moms certainly bring a special flavor to motherhood. Their approach is a light one that can often be undervalued. Parents are more often measured by whether their kids are well behaved than by the happiness in their homes. Perhaps in some cases our values are turned around. I think of the culture Jesus introduced into His inner circle—one where the people were criticized for eating and drinking too much, not observing the discipline of fasting, and not washing their hands before meals (Matt. 9:14; 11:19; 15:2). It sounds a lot like the criticism I have heard against Palm Tree moms, who are less uptight than most.

In these words from celebrity Palm Trees are some secrets to why children of Palm Tree moms may think they have a lucky break in growing up on Palm Beach:

I never really did years of movie-after-movie-after-movie, but when you've got three toddlers in the house, you're performing all day long anyway, with puppet shows and stories. I act around the clock.

Julia Roberts

She raised us with humor, and she raised us to understand that not everything was going to be great—but how to laugh through it.

Liza Minnelli on mom Judy Garland

When you're dying laughing because your three-year-old made a fart joke, it doesn't matter what else is going on. That's real happiness.

Gwyneth Paltrow

[What's beautiful about my mother is] her compassion, how much she gives, whether it be to her kids and grandkids or out in the world. She's got a sparkle.

Kate Hudson on mom Goldie Hawn

The Palm Tree Mom and Nurturing

What Harry says: Mommy made me a green birthday cake with sour-worm candy on it. It was so gross! She's cool. And she tickles me when she's angry. We both laugh and forget what I've done wrong.

What Vera says: Mommy kisses a lot. She lets me sit on her. She makes noises like all the animals. Her laugh is loud!

What her husband says: Jessica turned baby care into a game. She made jokes, rhymes, songs, and moves to go with things I thought were just drudgery. Sometimes, I'm sure, she'd rather be out with her friends, but she makes the kids her playmates for an hour or two every day and seems genuinely happy afterward. I've noticed that if the kids are happy, she is too.

The best thing is how she has made the spiritual nurturing of our kids come alive. Her physical presence, affection, and love have opened up our children's hearts to the love of God. They already know Jesus as a friend who loves them with all His heart, because she has shown them that. She definitely gives them a positive expectation in life.

Her openness about emotions has also taught them to show theirs and talk about them. She's taught us all that to build relationships, we have to feel things together.

What Jessica says about her Palm Tree mom: I remember a lot of pretend play. My mom never sold her old clothes; she just added them to my pile of dress-up outfits. She let me do her hair and makeup as well as my own. She was never ashamed to take me shopping with her no matter how ridiculously I had dressed for the outing.

My mom always had something delicious to eat, whether we were camping, sitting in church, or celebrating a birthday. She did not believe that kids should have a tough or boring time anywhere. She called the candy in her handbag "mood fixers" and dished them out when any one of her kids got a little cranky.

The Palm Tree Mom and Discipline

What Harry says: Mommy likes to give me stars and high fives when I eat all my veggies, and she gives me candy when I sit still in church. It's in her purse. She eats some too because she sits still too.

When I'm naughty, she sends me to the naughty chair, but it's okay because there is a toy box there to play with.

What her husband says: I can imagine her playing ring and run in the neighborhood with our kids one of these days. I may have to discipline the whole brood all by myself because she becomes a kid when she's with Harry and Vera. With Nicola, she's still the mommy, though.

She lives for today. I don't know how she's going to get the kids into a routine once they're all in school! She tries, but it makes her miserable.

"Kids have a wild imagination," she tells me every time I want to discipline them for lying. Harry and Vera can tell her any tall tale and she'll "believe" them, perhaps even adding a wilder episode to the story, just to let them know she adores them. Once they expose *her* confabulation, she turns the tables warmheartedly by saying something like "And I wonder if you were also trying to catch me with *your* story! You almost did! It was a great story. Now, I think I know what *really* happened."

Once Harry stole a candy bar from the cupboard. Jessica caught him red-handed. I would have given him a stern talking-to and a consequence. Jessica felt that being caught was bad enough and said Harry's big crocodile tears were proof that he was sorry. I thought he was just being manipulative. She believes the best about everyone.

What other moms say: When kids become mean to one another at a gathering, she'll quickly come up with an entertaining distraction instead of sorting out the guilty party. She seems to dislike the school's discipline system too. I don't think she'll allow the school to punish her children. If they are going to be excluded from an outing or kept after school for detention, I'm sure she'll talk the teachers out of it. She can use both charm and drama effectively.

She excuses some of her children's behavior by reminding everybody that they are just kids, but when her kids are mean to people or animals, she is firm about making them apologize and give hugs. Her kids are definitely taught to love and to share.

What Jessica says about her Palm Tree mom: My mom never spanked me like all the other moms of her generation did with their kids. She laughed too hard at my antics to keep a straight face. She did try, but that just cracked us up even more. When she really wanted to get across to me that she was not pleased, she would send me to the landing at the top of the stairs. It was a dreadfully boring place to sit alone. I hated it, so I guess it worked.

Criticism wasn't her style either. She'd rather point out all the good things about something. I knew what was wrong with it by what she *didn't* say. If she had to disapprove, she used humor. Once I wore a dress that was much too short. She made big eyes and remarked, "Well, you won't need to lift your skirt to visit the ladies' room, will you?"

The Palm Tree Mom and Training

What her husband says: Jessica likes to do things with the kids, so I'm not sure if they can do a whole lot for themselves yet. She still washes them, dresses them, helps them pick up toys now and then, and clears the table with them. She likes these physical mothering duties more than the "preachy-speechy" bits, as she calls the serious parenting. I think they need to do more chores, but she doesn't want to spoil their fun or interrupt their games.

She also tends to speak for them, especially for little Vera, our quiet one. She makes me think of the preschool teachers who are on the stage with the kids in the school play. These teachers do all the moves and coax the shy ones until everybody is participating. I think she'll always be physically involved with the kids and their activities. That is her way of training them.

What other moms say: She has so much energy! Her kids learn the fun way and by being exposed to places and people we don't have the courage to take our own kids to. She's forever on the go with them. By making Harry's schoolwork fun for him, we've seen her turn him into a good student.

What Jessica says about her Palm Tree mom: It was fun to be with my mom, so I watched her, joined in when she worked, and ended up learning to do almost everything a woman needs to know to run a household. I can't remember her ever giving me a list of instructions. She just said, "Wanna join me?" and whatever she was doing, I did. She had no issue with mistakes. She usually laughed at them, but in a way that made me feel relieved. This made me almost fearless to try out new things. To this day, I don't get upset if dresses tear, food burns, or cakes flop. She has taught me that everything can be tried more than once.

I try to do what she did. I spend a lot of time with the kids and take them with me whenever I can. I believe that life itself can be the best curriculum.

The Palm Tree Mom Coping with Life in General
What other mothers say: Jessica slimmed right down to her pre-baby weight in no time. It must be because

she's always moving and knows the latest fad diet. And she breastfed those babies for years. Motherhood seems to have made her even prettier and more alive. It's almost unfair.

Her kids seem happy, and the baby is always dressed up so cute when they go out. You can tell she has the energy to do all the things that we let slide when we are exhausted. She truly seems to be enjoying their diverse personalities, their quirks, and even their occasional naughty behavior.

What her husband says: Jessica is like a jack-in-the-box: she can't be kept down for long. Whatever challenges motherhood brings, she just bounces back. Even when Harry was hospitalized after breaking a leg, she didn't complain that it disrupted her life. She adapted to the short nights, pretended to love the hospital food so Harry would eat it too, and brightened everyone's day.

Our kids will know they are loved and adored. If they make mistakes in the years to come, she'll be there to help them find the silver lining. Her belief in a good future for them will make them believe in it too. They may need to do a whole lot of growing up, but for now Jessica seems to be more concerned with guarding their childhood than with getting them to act like adults.

What Harry says: Mommy dances a lot and swings her bottom and her arms. She's happy.

Are You a Palm Tree Mom?

You probably identify with the spunk and joy that Jessica spreads to her family. You will not share all her characteristics, and if life has dealt you a few more blows than it has dealt her, you may long for her innocence and childlike naïveté. If you are a bit older and wiser than she is, you may have lost the luxury of being "chirpy." Your parents may not have been as charmed by your Palm Tree antics as Jessica's mom was, and they may have trimmed your coconuts a little, leaving you a bit more serious about real life than Jessica is. Nevertheless, you will share some of the beautiful fruit that comes from the Natural Palm Tree Mom. When the stricter moms look at you as if you have missed the boat, toss your hair back and say:

- I see the best in my children.
- My kids know how to live life to the fullest.
- I set an example of gratitude and generosity.
- I raise kids who can find joy no matter what life throws at them.
- I don't expect my kids to act like grown-ups before they have grown up.
- I've never killed a childhood dream. I'm a dream giver.

Perhaps you want your children, spouse, or friends to know why your Palm Tree parenting style is so different from what they may regard as "the right way." You know by now it has pros and cons and doesn't work for everyone. Consider showing them your individualized Tall Trees Parenting Profile report so they can see you're not abnormal, just unconventional! It will list your valuable parenting strengths as well as pointers you need to keep in mind as you become an even greater mom.

Your challenges will be unique, depending on which elements of Boxwood, Rose, or Pine are present in your distinct "mixture," but any Palm Tree can consider working on the following points. Pick one or two, tell someone you're going to give the ideas a shot, and ask the person in a month or two if he or she sees your progress. Your willingness to try will be appreciated.

- I will make an effort to give you enough advance warning before I do something that will disrupt your routine or comfort.
- I will keep my impulsive promises (but I'll need you to remind me that I made them!).
- I will ask permission before I tell juicy stories about you or put you in the spotlight.
- I will give you more opportunities to speak your mind and will do my utmost to be quiet while you do.
- I will take your preferences about affection into account and not force hugs, kisses, and other forms of cuddling on you if it makes you uncomfortable.
- I will not try to cheer you up when you just need a minute to cry or vent frustration. I know that my optimism can feel like disrespect for your sadness.

Are You Living with a Palm Tree Mom?

The commitments of the Palm Tree mom listed above may bring up some hurt or laughter. Perhaps you have been scarred by your Natural

Palm Tree Mother, who never intended to hurt you but managed to do it anyway. Reread the list and consider the possibility that every one of her weaknesses could have a positive side in a different time and place.

We all have characteristics in our nature that clash with others' traits. If your Palm Tree mom or Palm Tree wife could live in a world that feels like Hawaii, she'd be in her element and would never hurt anyone. Perhaps her behavior offends you because her world falls far short of paradise.

May I introduce you to the world she was created for and dare you to make a space for her to share this world with you, even for just a few hours? Life can't always be ideal. However, with a Palm Tree, a little bit of paradise goes a long way to create a new dimension in your relationship. You may even enjoy it there. She'd want you to know:

I'm a happy Palm Tree in Hawaii when

- You give me room to explore and experiment. Don't spoil it for me with warnings and predictions. The surprise outcome—good or bad—is what I live for. I will learn from these experimental mistakes, not from articles or books about the issue.
- You let me enjoy the spotlight without accusing me of being conceited or trying to impress your friends. From the spotlight, I can get a positive message to more people. I'm after that, not the applause and adoration.
- You allow me regular visits to exciting places full of action and possibilities. You can stand on the sidelines if you don't want to swing from the chandeliers with

me. Just smile and wave. You'll be my hero for giving me an escape from my dry routine.

- You allow me to make you happy and spoil you a little (okay, a lot!). Don't check the price tag or bring up inflation when I go overboard with a gift. I'm a bargain hunter, so I probably got it on special anyway. If not, I'll save us a bunch of money elsewhere with my charm.

- You steer me away from temptation and danger without preaching at me. I can hear and follow your advice when it is given kindly. The more you tell me stories of gloom and doom, the more curious I become.

- You give me little notes, pictures, and handmade gifts. These convince me that you really like me. I need to be liked, not just loved. I need to know I make you happy, and proof helps a lot.

- You allow me to express my passion and excitement without pretending you don't know me. I will make an effort not to embarrass you, but look at the faces of the other people in these situations! They're laughing and smiling. I like doing that to people.

- You dream and fantasize with me. I live on possibilities and potential, wild ideas and even fairy tales. When you pull me into that world, it builds a lasting bond with you that we can't get by doing housework together.

- You touch and cuddle me. Of all my sense organs, my skin remembers the best that you love me. I sometimes forget lovely things you said or lose gifts you gave me, but the feeling of your arms around my neck and being loved passionately are what I go back to whenever I'm lost.

- You say the serious things in a way I can hear them. Touch me so I can remember that you're speaking from a point of love, and use humor to bring the point across. I will know you are serious. When you come down on me like a thunderstorm, I can't hear a thing.

- You focus on the positives. I can sit and nod and seem to be listening, but when everything is dark and serious, I'm really somewhere on a beach in the sunshine while you drone on. If you absolutely have to break bad news, please sandwich it for me between two really good things.

- You compliment how I look. I try hard, and appearances matter to me because beauty is one of the ways in which I bring joy to others. It's not vanity.

- You celebrate with me along the way, not just when all the work is done. Allow me to get excited about the chickens before they're hatched. There's no harm in my getting overly exhilarated, because when things don't work out I'll just bounce right back.

(Just one more thing: Yes, my love list may be longer than the other tree types' lists. It's not that I'm high maintenance; I'm just fluent in all the love languages. Even if you can speak only one, I'll feel loved. I just wanted to give you a lot of options. By the way, that is another love language that speaks to me: many options. Okay, I'm done.)

The Palm Tree Mom's First Step to (super)Natural Motherhood

Jessica's children and husband are not all like her. Especially Vera might find her mom to be somewhat loud and busy. As wonderful as Jessica is at being a friend to her children, other aspects of motherhood are naturally harder for her. There will be times when a frown cannot be tickled away or when your children will not respond to your love with a hug and a smile. There will also be times when your spouse disapproves of how you live your life. Instead of taking this as rejection, you could look deeper and discover a simple temperament mismatch. Your Tall Trees Parenting Profile will identify six aspects of your personality that will help you and your loved ones understand one another better.

Still, no matter how hard you try to meet everyone's needs, you just aren't perfect, and neither is anyone else. The following confessions of a Natural Palm Tree Mom will not all apply to you, but keep them handy as a peace offering for those days when your spouse or children are less than pleased and you are big enough to acknowledge that you need God's help. Admitting this is your first step to becoming a (super)Natural Mom.

I realize I might annoy you when
- I talk so much that you don't get an opportunity to speak your piece.
- I get a little overexcited about new things that are coming, forgetting the good in what I already have.
- I use charm and the gift of the gab to wiggle myself out of responsibilities.

- I say yes to too many people and projects at the same time and end up neglecting you.
- I don't play by the rules, getting myself or even you into trouble.
- I forget to be myself and instead put on whatever persona pleases the crowd. This makes me seem false, doesn't it?
- I move into your personal life and space without your permission.
- I ignore warnings about people and end up in partnerships and relationships that are harmful.
- I get messy and disorganized to the point that it affects your life as well.
- I make hasty promises to you that I don't fulfill.
- I seek the adoration of people to the point where I might compromise my values.
- I make light of things that are serious for you and joke to relieve tension rather than resolving problems with you.
- I impulsively say and do things that can't always be mended by an apology.
- I waste time, money, and energy on unnecessary things and therefore miss the more important priorities.
- I shift the blame or make creative excuses instead of owning up to my mistakes.
- I disrupt your plans by not thinking ahead.
- I fail to keep your personal details and secrets to myself, causing you embarrassment.

- I am not scared of mistakes and end up making many.
- I let you off the hook in the name of grace instead of letting you learn from painful consequences.
- I apologize easily but quickly make the same mistake again, leaving you to think I am not sincerely sorry. (I am!)

One more thing: forgive me for sometimes wanting something that is more fun than us, when we truly are a God idea.

A Palm Tree Mom's Reflection of God's Heart

Jessica puts many things on a lampstand to shine on everyone, especially her **joy** (Mark 4:21). When her joy is in God and based on knowing she is a favored daughter of the Most High God (something she regularly says out loud), she spreads this joy to her children. They will learn from her never to allow their joy to be stolen by unfortunate events (Neh. 8:10).

Love is not love unless it is shown and expressed. God insists on our making our love tangible and visible. Jessica's name means "God sees" and "rich." Jessica exhibits this **generosity** by giving herself, her body, her belongings, her time, and her encouraging words in a way that enriches people. In this she is much like the father of the Prodigal Son, who hugged, kissed, gifted, and celebrated him (Luke 15:20–24).

Jessica's **forgetfulness** has its beautiful side: she forgets especially the mistakes and the sins of the past. Her children will experience in this the forgetfulness of a forgiving God, who promises that our confessed sin is drowned in the deep sea and banished from all His records (Mic. 7:18–19).

She has **openheartedness** that extends beyond people she knows to those who are not in her world: strangers and even "unlovable" people. We see this in God when He says from the time of Abraham that He intends to include all nations in His blessing (Gen. 22:18). Palm Trees are not gatekeepers but rather includers, who bring everyone along for the feast whenever there is one. Because of this, her children are likely to view God as a yes-God with open heart and open arms who will love them to wholeness.

Palm Trees often have **childlike faith**. Some may call them optimists, but Jessica's children know she's more than that. She has a faith that doesn't ask a lot of questions. It grasps a vision and runs with it. It is grounded in a proper perspective of knowing she is the child and God is the Father. She doesn't need to know or understand everything, because she knows He does. If He says that something will happen, Jessica doesn't doubt it for a minute.

Hope can often be mistaken for optimism too. Jessica is a hopeful person. Hope involves a deliberate choice to expect more good than bad to come from an uncertain situation. Jessica chooses hope so consistently that it is part of her character. It makes her expect the best from her children. It helps her give them the benefit of the doubt and encourages them to believe in the good God has for them in this world and the next. Hope like this is contagious because it sees what God is able to do and not just what He has already done. Jessica has the kind of Hebrews 11 faith that uses godly imagination and hopes without demanding proof! Her children will dream big dreams with a big God because she teaches them how.

For Reflection

1. How does your Palm Tree temperament shine through your mothering? How has mothering matured you?

2. What are the greatest challenges that being a mom poses to the lifestyle you value? How do you cope with these challenges?

3. Has anyone ever criticized you for being too permissive with your kids? How might you kindly deflect the criticism?

4. Pick five words that describe your character. What positive values do these traits model for your children?

5. Name a Palm Tree trait that your child finds overwhelming. Then name a habit you can cultivate to temper that trait in a way that honors your child's needs.

6

The (un)Natural Mom in the Rose Bush Garden

When looking for a tree type to represent this temperament, I searched for one that was hardy in nature: prickly but also productive. A cactus initially came to mind, as this plant seems able to survive in the most hostile environments without failing to flower spectacularly in season. One would not want to insult this personality type by calling her a cactus, however! Rose bushes were my second choice. They are thorny enough yet known for their exceptional flowers. A properly pruned rose bush has many positive traits.

Some celebrities have roses named after them. Eleanor Roosevelt made a typical Rose Bush remark about the rose named after her, but it happens to be a bit too "sharp" to publish here. The possibility of fame and success is a special package Rose Bush babies receive at birth. Those rosettes that were pinned onto the chest of champions in the old days are what Rose Bushes want. A Rose Bush has drive and competitiveness ingrained in her nature.

Unfortunately, most Roses also have thorns. Their parents can usually attest to the fact that they were hard to shape. The closer you get, the more you encounter the thorns. The children of Rose Bush parents might complain about this trait too.

The Rose Bush temperament corresponds strongly with the choleric temperament, as well as with the personality type D (dominant, direct, decisive) in the DiSC indicator. If you are familiar with these and other indicators, you can read with this in mind.

A Day in the Life of Megan

Before we enter Megan's world, a word to fellow Rose Bush moms: your whole history plays a part in how much good, bad, or ugly of your temperament you display on any given day. Rose Bushes aren't always in full bloom. When tended with care, they explode in generous fragrance and color. When pests and adverse environmental factors hit, however, such moms can bear more thorns than flowers. Over the years, many challenges have eaten away at Megan, and she has not quite recovered from them all. The description of Megan is given on a day when her petals are pale. Therefore, you will not identify with all of her traits, even if your Tall Trees Parenting Profile says you're for sure a Rose Bush.

Many Rose Bush moms will read Megan's story and feel they are rosier and less prickly than she is. Perhaps their parents did a more persistent pruning job than Megan's did. Megan has been allowed to "shrub" unchecked for many years. Her mother prayed that Megan's strong first husband would continue what Megan's parents had left undone in this regard, but Megan left him after three years because they couldn't share the power in the household in a productive fashion. She ended up marrying Box-Pine David, who owns watering cans and gloves but no clippers and shears. Going against her wishes has not worked out for him. He lets her be. It works for both of them.

Megan just turned forty-eight. She doesn't mind admitting her age. It shows that she's accomplished a few things in life and helps people not to underestimate her. She looks forty. When asked about her first marriage, she says only, "It was a mistake." She has moved on with her son Kevin, who is now eighteen. She married David when Kevin was six. Their second son, Josh, is ten.

5:00 a.m. *In bed* The alarm clock announces the start of the race. Megan flies out of bed. She has an hour's head start on the rest of the household. She loves that. She can get a bunch done before she needs to deal with her family's barrage of needs. She dresses swiftly and puts on foundation but will apply the rest of her makeup in the car on the way to work. She keeps the essentials in her glove box.

6:00 a.m. *In the kitchen* The news is all predictable. She knew that China would do what China just announced they had done. She told everyone it was coming but no, they thought a woman speaking about international politics should mind her own business. Ha! She is minding her own lucrative business, thank you very much! Lucrative because she has a gut of gold. She feels things. Like she now feels that her husband and youngest have overslept again. It's not her job to go upstairs to salvage the situation, but she can't leave it to them to get ready on time. She hurriedly takes them their breakfast and a stern look, then gets everything else ready in a flash.

She manages everyone through the morning processes while texting instructions to her assistant, emailing her business partner in California, and reading the morning paper.

7:05 a.m. *In the car* She is ready to go. The kids are not. She pulls out of the driveway as Josh frantically emerges from the front door, waving an empty lunch box he hasn't had time to fill. She shrugs and wears the smile that is not a smile, because it means, "You know your problems aren't my problems." She paraphrases it more gently as he flops into the backseat: "Remember we agreed that we will leave on time whether you have everything or not?" He can complete the speech she's not making this time: *You're not underfed, so one day without your lunch will certainly not kill you.* She knows he will find something to eat. She does not wish a hungry day on him; she just doesn't want to budge on the boundary that she feels is fair.

She makes it halfway to school before remembering that this time in the car with kids is supposed to be treasured. She turns off the radio and asks what their day holds. There is a sudden gasp from Kevin, who remembers he has a basketball game after school and was supposed to bring his gear along. Megan glances into the rearview mirror with a question mark on her face. He replies, "No problem, Mom. Just remembered something."

Her standard reply: "And have you made a plan?"

"Yes, Mom."

She feels proud. She has taught her sons to be solution minded rather than problem minded. Josh still seems a bit too dependent for a ten-year-old, though.

7:55 a.m. *At the office* She's just in time. She likes the feeling of things running like clockwork. Someone made fairly decent coffee. She can grab a cup and get down to business.

8:00 a.m. *At the office* A text message comes in from Leanne. Jessica has changed their meeting time. Megan can roll with the punches, but Jessica is making a habit of disrespecting her. Megan texts Jessica to let her know that this will be the last time she responds favorably to a last-minute cop-out. Megan draws a few wild arrows in her electronic diary to show what will go where and quickly updates her schedule. *What do I have an assistant for if I still have to do all of this myself?* she wonders.

9:30 a.m. *In her corner office* Megan glances over at the picture of her hero from the TV drama *Suits* and reads his famous quote out loud: "Work until you no longer need to introduce yourself." She'll settle for her name on the company board in the foyer. She sits down and notices the family picture on the corner of her desk. It is six years old. The boy smiling with milk teeth in the picture now has grown-up front teeth, and the scrawny kid who was all knees is now a buff teen who shaves every morning. *It goes fast*, she thinks. She likes them growing up, though. She calls her assistant to ask her to book a session to have new family pictures taken as soon as possible. Her assistant's phone is off, of course. She'll do it herself. She gets to work on the proposal for the postponed meeting.

11:15 a.m. *In the boardroom* Jessica, Leanne, and another team member meet with Megan about their new project's timeline. Megan wants things wrapped up by March. Jessica is convinced it can be done, but Leanne pleads for more time to research the costs. The meeting is done in twenty minutes. Megan feels invigorated by such quick results.

11:35 a.m. *In her corner office* Megan dives right back into her work and never takes a break until Jessica knocks and brings her a smoked-chicken salad and coffee the way she likes it. Jessica looks eager to tell her a juicy bit of news. Megan lowers her head to signal that she's not in the mood.

Megan has been taking her lunch in her office for a while now. She can't see the point of socializing in the break room. She can work through lunch and make up for leaving early enough to still have time for family. She may make an exception tomorrow because it will be her birthday. Megan prefers a stylish dinner or a visit to a unique site, but she allows Jessica to go overboard with streamers and cake once a year, as it seems to do wonders for the morale of the entire office when they can make a little fun of Megan and force her to wear a party hat.

After more than an hour of uninterrupted work, her cell phone beeps. The text from Josh says, "Mom, is it okay to come pick me up now, or are you busy?" She was supposed to be at school already! Fortunately, she can get there in less than ten minutes. This Boxwood kid gets stressed easily, so she texts back that she's on her way.

She slams a file with instructions a little too forcefully onto Jessica's desk, making her spill nail polish. Megan ignores this. She grabs four new files from the in-basket and slips them under her arm. She's contorted around all the things she's carrying by the time she reaches the car. She pops her high heels into the trunk along with the briefcase and files. She slides into her leather seat, her driving shoes, and her rush mode in a single smooth motion.

3:15 p.m. *Back at the school* Josh's lip is quivering. Megan holds up a forbidding hand and shakes her head even before he gets in. "First calm down. We'll talk when you can control your tears." To give him a few minutes to regain the self-control that suits his age, she turns up the radio and listens to the financial indicators and then the traffic report. Finally Josh has the opportunity to say that there was a strange car outside the school and he really didn't feel safe while waiting.

Megan is no longer unsympathetic. She wants a detailed description of that car. If someone is stalking children, she will do something about it! She calms herself down and then tries to put Josh at ease. "The bottom line is you are safe and I was only ten minutes late. I'm sorry you were scared." She tries to imagine what he felt like, but she has a hard time thinking like a child. She is angry that in just ten minutes her child could have been a target. She will call the school tomorrow to have a warning issued, and she'll never be late again. She'll make a Plan B with a full-time mom who could keep an eye on Josh if Megan is ever late again.

3:30 p.m. *At home* She hugs Josh as he gets out of the car. He looks surprised but relieved and starts crying. "I thought you were going to tell me to suck it up and move on." Megan can't recall saying those exact words to him before, but they sound like her, she admits to herself. Josh clearly expects little empathy from her. She feels bad.

"No, I owed you a hug. I really should have been on time. I'll do better. I'll be early tomorrow, okay?"

When Josh looks much calmer, she announces that homework needs to be done and back in the schoolbag by bedtime. If Josh has questions about the homework, he can ask Kevin when he gets home.

Megan grabs an energy drink from the fridge. She's going to have an afternoon run. She changes in five minutes and hits the road with earbuds in. She's glad to have a son like Josh who behaves when she's out.

4:30 p.m. *At home* Megan arrives back from her run just as Kevin leaps from his friend's car, shouting a team credo. "We won, Mom!" he calls before remembering to act cool at all times.

"I'd hope so. You certainly have put in enough hours on the court to come out tops eventually."

"Mom, can we not make everything about hard work?"

"Fine, let's make it about lazy losing, then."

Kevin backs off. He keeps a witty comeback to himself because he needs to ask a favor. "Mom, this win puts us in the play-offs in Aspen this weekend. Can you take me, please? I really don't want to take the stuffy bus with all the juniors." Megan has a rule that Kevin can't drive or catch a ride with friends for distances longer than a hundred miles without an adult in the car. This has been embarrassing to him and is what has him traveling with the younger students.

"We'll have to leave at five Saturday morning and return immediately after the game; otherwise I can't. I'm sorry. I have a function at seven that night." This is going to cost her a lot of time, but she makes this sacrifice gladly. She believes that the children should be supported at all times.

5:10 p.m. *In the kitchen* Kevin has crammed everything that was in the fridge between two slices of bread. "Hey, that will be seven dollars, thank you!" Megan alerts him to his excess. He gets the message, pulls out three slices of jack cheese, and returns them to the resealable bag.

"Happy?"

"No, Kevin." She pretends to be strict now, but her smile reveals that she secretly loves messing with him. He is fast and feisty. Josh can't handle her jabs; neither can David. She even occasionally enjoys being bowled over by his arguments. She wants to send a confident son into the world.

She runs up the stairs and past Josh's room for a quick shower, startling Josh sitting at his desk. "What?" she calls.

"You're doing that thing again, Mom! You're running like when we had the fire."

"Not again," she moans. Josh was four when a gas heater set the bedroom on fire. She ran up and down the stairs, first with a fire extinguisher and then with blankets. Everyone else just froze. Instead of remembering her quick footsteps as those of a fearless firefighter, he finds them scary. The psychologist said that after trauma, a sound or smell can take someone right back into the fear of the moment. Megan thinks it's all a little much.

"Josh, I sometimes have to run. I'm sorry it stresses you. Try to breathe like the doctor showed you. If you don't smell smoke, everything is fine, okay?" She doesn't wait to see if this does the trick, because if it doesn't, she has nothing more.

In the shower, she prays for Josh with passion and faith that God will be as real a fortress to him as He is to her. She remembers her own fear of water after a near drowning when she was nine. God took it away without her realizing when He did it. She ends her prayer with a confession: "Lord, I forget so easily that I need You and that I need to pray. I just carry on without You. I want to learn to come to You even when my world is not shaking. I just forget. Help me. Give me wisdom."

6:00 p.m. *In the kitchen* David is back from work and scans the kitchen for signs of dinner. Megan is watching a taped episode of *Power Couple*. She'd love to compete in a reality series. She's planning to whip up dinner fast once she's done here. David sighs and decides to make something from scratch for a change. Megan hears him getting busy but pretends not to. It's his turn, for sure, and he likes cooking more than she does.

An hour later, David calls everyone to the table, but Kevin is just starting his homework and asks to take his plate upstairs. Josh would like to watch TV. David is about to give in when Megan firmly says, "Dad made a special dinner. You will respect that. Let's sit down." She wishes she could order them to also have deep family chats, but they never developed that culture. The conversations are about work, schoolwork, homework, housework, and yard work. Everyone is listening, and she is delegating. A part of her feels relieved that they never have piercing conversations about how they would respond if one of them got cancer or whether they should prepare for the apocalypse. She avoids speculation and drama.

After dinner they all clean up together, but Megan does most of it. David cooked, after all. She does it faster anyway. They each head off to what they were doing before dinner.

After crafting a presentation to promote her new idea, Megan watches the 10:00 p.m. news but comments about every point so passionately that David can't focus on the book he's reading. She glances at him and wonders how people can check out of a world where Rome—and sometimes your own city—is burning down to read about a fantasy world and the adventures of people who aren't even real.

She never said good night to the kids, but they are big enough now not to need a tucking in. Occasionally she misses the hugs. Perhaps Josh needed one tonight. Perhaps she did.

10:30 p.m. *In bed* David and Megan are each in their own world. Most nights she's still processing work-related concerns and the week's challenges, but tonight she reflects on the year that has passed. Tomorrow she has a new beginning and wants to open up her heart more. "Dinner was lovely," she says. She tries to think of something even more appreciative but fears she may sound phony. Many minutes pass and she almost falls asleep.

"I've always wanted to write my own book," David says. "Something that would be a classic one day. I think the title might be *When Love Trumps Truth: The Danger of Fundamentalism.* What do you think?"

"David! You never told me this. It's close to midnight, and suddenly you tell me this important thing when I'm half-asleep. Why?"

"This is the only hour of the day when you're not armed, Meg. Tonight you checked your weapons and your laptop at the door before coming to bed. You felt safe to talk to."

His words melt her heart. She wraps around him. Tomorrow she'll try not to strap her armor back on. It will be her birthday, after all.

Rose Bush through the Seasons of Motherhood

A lady at Megan's church keeps calling her Career Woman. Megan resents the implication that she may not be a good mom. To prove this lady wrong, she volunteered to write a guide for prospective moms at their church.

David calls her "often mistaken but never in doubt." She is certain that what she wrote in this guide is the way to do motherhood.

Deciding to Start a Family

Mother will be one of the most consuming roles you as a woman could ever play. Make sure parenthood is what you want. It is quite all right to postpone this until you have achieved other goals. Remember the places you've always wanted to go, the famous people you want to rub shoulders with, and the physical feats and adventures you want to tick off your bucket list before settling down. Once you are content that you have gotten the most out of your youth, you are ready to contemplate starting a family.

When you feel ready for children, make sure your husband agrees. Have a rational and well-planned argument with a few solid points when you put this on the table. The idea may scare him initially, so be the fearless one for both your sakes. If he initiates this conversation before you are ready, remind him that you will be the one most impacted by the changes; your body, your health, your career, your sleep, and your future will be altered in every single way. Convince him to wait until you both are ready.

An important issue to iron out well in advance is the decision to be a stay-at-home mom. It's not for everyone. Know yourself well enough to be honest about where you stand. If you're wired to be employed outside the home, decide how long you'll take off from work. Also discuss this with your employer.

Read Proverbs 31 again. This prudent wife ran an import and export business, a textile and clothing design factory, and more. She did this while taking care of her household. You can too.

Pregnancy and Birth

Pregnancy is a sacrifice. The sooner you realize that, the better. Your body will change forever. In exchange, however, you will receive the greatest reward imaginable: a brand-new life to hold in your hands.

Try to be well informed, and verify that those who prepare you for birth are qualified experts in their field. But don't get stuck on information overload. You don't need old wives' tales and wisdom from a bygone age, and you don't need a million rules to follow; you need just the latest advice in a nutshell so you can make your own choices. Make decisions for yourself and stick to them. It's okay to pick a new doctor or midwife if your current caregivers seem to want to change your mind for you. Starting motherhood with confidence will help you through the tough days after the birth. Start right!

Avoid those endless lists of things you supposedly need to buy and organize far in advance. This causes undue stress, especially that hospital bag! Your mom, a girlfriend, or your husband can always get whatever you may have missed while packing. Set up your "nursery" whenever and wherever it is most convenient for you. Not everything needs to match either. Be practical. No one has ever blamed badly coordinated baby room décor for any permanent psychological issues! Stick to essentials.

Baby Days

This phase is not easy. One can quickly lose control. Remind yourself that you are the adult. Review the difficult things you have mastered in your life so far and think positively. If you could learn to drive, study, and work with money, you can learn to be a mom. You'll survive.

Some moms are fulfilled by motherhood alone. You may not be such a mom. It is all right to admit it. Find some significance outside of the home. Take your baby with you. Keep making an impact on your community. Get out a lot. Remain informed about life around you. There is nothing worse than a circle of young moms discussing nothing but diaper rash and remedies for engorgement.

If you feel trapped by your baby, you might take out your frustration on her or even your husband. Give your whole heart, body, and attention to your little one when she needs you, but don't assume she needs you every minute of every day and night. Don't build all your worth on her. That isn't mothering; it's smothering.

Asking for help is hard, but when it's offered, take it. Many tasks can be handled by older siblings and your husband, a good friend, or a carefully selected child-care provider while you take care of important matters. Don't let others do everything, though. Keep the significant aspects of your baby's care firmly in your own hands. You remain the primary parent.

Don't discuss breastfeeding, sleeping arrangements, and other contentious topics unless you want many conflicting opinions. If you've made up your mind about how you want to go about something, don't be swayed. Just say, "We won't all agree about these things. Let's each do whatever works for us."

Try to stay active and fit. Parenting is no excuse for looking or dressing sloppily. Keep your dignity.

Toddler Training

This is where the game is lost or won for the long haul. You need to establish who the authority in the home is. Make sure your toddler knows it's you and your husband. Never tell a child to wait for their punishment until Daddy comes home. This sends the dangerous message that you are powerless and Daddy is the executioner.

Little ones need to understand early on that they can't always have their own way, that they will not always have three options to choose from, and that you are armed and dangerous even when you don't seem to be. Prove this by speaking calmly one time, then acting decisively if they don't obey at once.

Never stoop to the level of the pleading parent. Try not to lose your cool. Sometimes fear gets children to obey, but it won't work when they're older. Respect lasts longer. Prove to them that you are worthy of your authority. Calm confidence brings that message across the best.

Stick to your guns no matter how high the tantrums register on the Richter scale, even in public. Outlast your children. You're the adult! God gave you a weight advantage for a reason. You can take them out of a bath or strap them into a car seat when it's the best thing for them, with or without their agreeing to it. Many years will pass before they understand that you went against their wishes because you love them. You can't reason with toddlers.

School Years

You should enjoy parenting a lot more now than you did during the baby years. School-age kids have language, can be reasoned with, and usually sleep through the night! Another great thing about this phase is that kids start doing many things for themselves. They are not home as many hours of each day. You start getting most of your life and body back, which means you are more fulfilled, less frustrated, and probably a much more pleasant person to live with. Don't feel guilty about hours spent away from your children; just make them count so that once you're back home with your family, you have a lot left to give them.

These years are crucial for your children's futures. Pay close attention to such things as bullies and parents who hijack opportunities to which your children are entitled. Fight for your children until they are old enough to fight for themselves. Don't allow teachers to bully your kids either. Your hard work to make your children believe in themselves should not be destroyed by anybody. You pay the teachers' salaries. Insist on the best education.

As for achievement, no children should be left to think that anything but their best is acceptable. Love them unconditionally, but be firm with lazy or self-indulgent kids. Life will not put up with freeloaders; neither should you. Attend their sporting events and other activities so that you can identify areas in which your children may need extra coaching. Give it your all from your side as well.

School is about developing skills; skills are about gaining independence and employability; employability and independence guarantee greater chances of success in life. Make sure your children understand this. Kids respond best to high expectations.

Parenting Teens

You may no longer have the advantage of being physically stronger than your kids. You now have to work harder to earn the right to tell your teens what to do. You earn this right by being wise and reasonable, never spiteful.

Know more about drugs and the Internet than they do. Stay one step ahead. Maintain a firm hold on their activities, their curfews, their friends, their access to online social media, and their money, and keep them away from dangerous places and anything else that may lead them into trouble. Give them just enough money to sense what it can buy and also what it feels like when they have wasted it. Let them experience the weight of their mistakes. Never rescue them from the natural lessons of life.

While giving them less freedom than you would give an adult, you should start introducing adult responsibilities and skills. Prepare them for independent living.

Don't allow your teens to be sullen or snooty. Hormones are no excuse for this. Do you want your daughter to use her time of the month as an excuse for snapping at her boss one day? Teach your kids to own their anger, frustration, and other emotions and to rein them in. Emotional immaturity is an unattractive trait in young adults.

Letting Go

You should start practicing this from their first day of school or children's church. You should go away for weekends with your husband, leaving the children in a trusted adult's care. Go away for longer periods when they're older without calling every day. All these times away from one another grow a healthy independence in your children (and in you).

The first major test of letting go will come when your children face life-altering decisions, such as choosing career paths, starting with the choice of colleges and the like. These options are too important to risk all the money and time that may be wasted. Make these decisions with them rather than leaving them to make indelible mistakes. You are older and wiser for a reason. They may initially rebel but are likely to thank you one day for not letting them chase their whimsical childhood dreams blindly.

Decide at what age or stage of independence you regard your children as ready to leave the home. Prepare them for it. Remind them now and then how much time they have left to plan for their adult lives away from your home. If you happen to have a child who could have played a leading role in the movie *Failure to Launch*, enroll him in a program for such young adults, or at least make him get a job to pay his own way.

As for their choices of spouses, be honest about what you see in their love interests. Love is blind, and if you don't point out the flaws of unsuitable partners, your kids could regret it forever. Be specific and use concrete examples when exposing the other individuals' behavior. Your kids' spouses will raise your grandchildren and be your family forever. This alone gives you the right to have your say.

When your children have left your home physically and financially, you have to respect them as their own people. Then it is time to stop interfering.

"Granny Rose" Years

A grandma is an important coeducator of her grandchildren, but it is not necessary that you allow your children to delegate their responsibilities to you. You have made the sacrifices of parenting over the years in raising them, and now it is their turn. By all means help, babysit, host them all for Christmas, and bake cakes for the birthday parties, but have firm boundaries in place. You are not a surrogate parent.

You are still older and wiser. Therefore, when your children make serious mistakes with your grandchildren, you have the right to say what you think they should be doing. They might or might not follow your good advice, but your conscience will be clear.

Post this powerful quote from Eleanor Roosevelt where you can regularly remind yourself that parenthood is not your whole life and that you are no longer the center of your children's existence:

"You can never really live anyone else's life, not even your child's. The influence you exert is through your own life, and what you've become yourself."[1]

Megan found out that the guide was never given to mothers in their church. She was furious but concluded that the mommy who had to approve it must have seen in the principles too many failures in herself and probably took it personally. Megan still feels that one should be more objective and acknowledge that the guide could have helped many moms avoid the pitfalls of common parenting mistakes.

The Natural Rose Bush Mom

There's a blooming, pretty side to Megan, if you've not been able to see it yet. The mothering strengths of a Rose Bush mom have brought us some of the most influential men and women in the history of the world. They have brought about changes in mind-sets and have been like prophets who point out the need for transformation.

Here are quotes from some successful people of our time who give credit to certain Rose Bush moms for what they naturally and perhaps unconventionally deposited into their children's lives:

I had a very strong-willed mother, who I totally adored. She was always in control of her life.

Jan de Bont, film director

To describe my mother would be to write about a hurricane in its perfect power. Or the climbing, falling colors of a rainbow.

Maya Angelou, writer and civil rights activist

The greatest lesson that Mom ever taught me was this one: she told me there would be times in your life when you have to choose between being loved and being respected. She said to always pick being respected.

Chris Christie, politician

Barack Obama's mother, Stanley Ann Dunham, had quite an interesting life, shot through with coincidences. Stanley Ann was some mom—and by "some mom," it's meant that she was a globetrotting, oil-rep-marrying, CIA-front-employed, twelve-language-speaking, International Mom of Mystery.

Mondo Frazier, *The Secret Life of Barack Hussein Obama*

In the *New York Times* obituary, Hillary Clinton reminisced about her late mother, Dorothy Rodham. A memory stood out from when she was four years old and victimized by a neighborhood bully. "You have to face things and show them you're not afraid," her mother had told her, and that if she were hit again, "hit her back." Clinton "credited her mother with giving her a love of the higher learning that Mrs. Rodham never had, a curiosity about a larger world" than the one her mom had seen, "and a will to persevere," about which she said her mother knew a great deal.[2]

The Rose Bush Mom and Nurturing

What her kids say: Mom is not exactly the touchy-feely type, but she carried us when we were going too slowly in the shops and put us on her lap in the movie theaters so we could see over people's heads. She cuddled us for a bit when we had a nightmare or a fever. Sometimes we may have actually pretended to be sick when we were already feeling a lot better, just for one of those special cuddles.

Mom has a way of getting you to do what you should be doing, even when you don't feel like it. If not for her, we probably never would bathe regularly or brush our teeth properly.

What other moms say: Her kids are so easy. Perhaps it's because their every wish was never her command. They can handle many tough situations because they just never had that security net of a hovering parent. Megan's kids self-nurture. She taught them to.

Megan is a whirlwind of force. She was always able to breastfeed, cook, and get everyone dressed all at the same time. One got the impression she wasn't very nurturing until you looked closer and saw that their every need was taken care of. It just happened faster and more efficiently so that you didn't see her fussing with a child for hours like we did.

What her husband says: I did quite a bit of the baby care. I didn't mind. I had the patience for it. Megan really struggled to take the time to pat and bounce a baby three ways to get a painful burp out. I thought it a worthwhile challenge and got great at it. She laughs at such a challenge. To her, finding a multimillion-dollar deal is a challenge to stay up half the night for, not a burp. But when the kids had a true emergency, like when

Kevin had a concussion, she moved into his room and stayed up, took his vitals every hour, and functioned like a resident neurologist. I think she sees the real needs instead of responding to every little whine.

The Rose Bush Mom and Discipline

What Kevin says: We don't mess with Mom. She makes the rules and she speaks them only once. Sometimes we feel there are exceptions that she should take into account, but she really isn't one to negotiate. By the time you have your explanation ready to appeal your sentence, she's already executing justice.

Mom doesn't give silly consequences. She thinks about them carefully to make sure we will learn from them. The same goes for rewards. I once asked if I could get money as a reward for being obedient. She answered, "Only if I get paid for stopping at the red light." I got the point. Mom is always clear.

What Josh says: She sees us as grown-ups. She forgets that I am only ten. She always says, "Imagine you doing this at work. Your boss would fire you!" I once told her that I'm going to start working when I'm twenty. I don't know why, but that totally made her flip.

We try not to cry when we are punished. Mom thinks it's just drama when we cry. You can't make her feel sorry for you by crying. She doesn't buy it. If she said no, it stays no.

What her husband says: I sometimes feel I have to be a bit of an equalizer: she adds the law; I add grace. I think I sometimes undermine her discipline. I rethink, renegotiate, restate the rule that was broken, and try to arrive at a peaceful solution. She'll announce that there is no TV for a week, and then, when she travels five days later, I'll find a way to give the kids two days off their sentence. I noticed that takes us backward, not forward, and I look up to her for her resolve. She once chimed in during such a peacemaking effort and said, "We are not the United Nations or the Peace Corps; we are a household with principles."

The Rose Bush Mom and Training

What Kevin says: She is not keen on questions. When she tells you what to do but you don't quite get it, you better pretend and just move fast. You have to look confident while you do it or she will ask you what's wrong. I did a part-time job over the holidays with a boss like that. He made all the other students nervous. I was used to performing under pressure and loved the job. It's that thing again about being prepared for real life. My mom does that so well.

She tells you what to do, leaves, and checks up afterward to see if you did it right. I'm okay with it. My mom and I both think teamwork slows us down.

She really can be tough, but it's been a long time since I've had any punishment, because she let me have it when I was little, and I learned from it. We're almost friends now. She even lets me fight her a little. It's like verbal arm wrestling.

A great thing about my mom is how much money she gives us. She wants us to learn to work with it. She says that if she gives us so little that wasting it doesn't hurt and saving it doesn't hold a huge reward, we won't learn anything. Once when I was on the way to the mall, I lost all the money I had saved up for an iPad. She didn't give me one dollar of it back. I never put money in my pants pockets again.

What Josh says: You get into trouble when she gives you a job and you don't do it really, really well. My brother once put gift wrap and a ribbon around a bowl of salad to be sarcastic because Mom told him the previous salad wasn't "wrapped up nicely." Mom lost it.

My mom sees my talents before I do and makes sure I develop them to the max. She believes in me more than I do. It gives me guts to try new things.

What her husband says: Her high expectations are paying off. Our kids usually make it onto the team in the sports they love. They learned drive from her.

When there's work to be done, she makes sure everyone gets their orders, executes them to the bitter end, and does so to the best of their abilities. As a result, the kids know how to follow through, even with unpleasant chores.

What other moms say: Her kids could do a gazillion tough things before they were in primary school. They had to just figure it out. They don't get the best grades, as she simply refuses to do their projects for them. "They have to make their own rain," she says. She is at every game they play, but I've never seen her baby them. She has this way of getting them to take responsibility for their lives.

The Rose Bush Mom Coping with Life in General

What other moms say: She has it all: the good kids, the nice house, the prestigious job. She drives everywhere with those kids, serves on committees, rallies for causes, and still manages a household. She also runs. She's the ultimate superwoman.

I don't know if she's every kid's ideal mother. If she'd had a little girl with a tender heart, I think she'd have scarred her a little. God knows which kid to give to which parent, I guess! She was exactly the right mom to keep Kevin on track after the divorce. The child became incredibly defiant. She channeled all his aggression into extreme sports. It changed him for the better.

What her husband says: Megan is an extremely efficient mom. She's a lot like an alligator that lays her eggs on warm compost heaps so the incubation can continue without her constant presence. She finds ways to make sure the kids are taken care of at all times, even when she can't be there. Alligators carry their young in their jaws. Anyone who's ever tried to harm our children has found Megan's sharp teeth exposed. She fights for us.

She really is the nicest to the kids when she's had a challenging but successful day at work or has had a chance to spend all her energy on strenuous exercise. Work and sweat, not home, seem to determine her well-being.

I think letting go, despite what she wrote in that mothers' guide, is going to be hard for her. She likes to be in control and "in the know."

Are You a Rose Bush Mom?

You might not see much of yourself in Megan because you are a mixture of Rose Bush and a "gentler" tree. Still, being part of the circle of Natural Rose Bush Moms is something to be proud of. Hopefully you were able to notice Megan's many strengths as a mother and can add some of your own from your Tall Trees Parenting Profile.

Here are some affirmations to keep in mind when you feel like an (un)Natural Mom:

- I work hard at preparing my children for real life.
- I am honest with my children about them and myself.
- I motivate my children to live up to their potential.
- I set an example of hard work and perseverance.
- I teach my children submission to authority.
- I act with authority and confidence.
- I am responsible with my kids.

God's way of working with Rose Bushes tends to be as tough as the plant. So when you humbly admit that the following aspects of motherhood need work, be ready to be changed in an uncomfortable way. Never doubt that God loves you enough to take you through the purifying furnace (Mal. 3:2–3). How we operate in relationships is the most important refinement and therefore the hardest. Let God direct you to choose one or more of those challenges listed on your report or any of these commitments:

- I will focus on intentional nurturing during mealtimes, bedtime, bath time, traveling time, and weekends.
- I will put my work aside to connect with my children in their own worlds, starting with finding out all of their favorites, from colors to songs and movies.
- I will stop insisting that my way is the best and only way and will intentionally identify the value in how my children do things differently.
- I will read a book or attend a course on emotional intelligence, listening to children, or managing my anger, whichever is my current challenge.
- I will confess and ask for forgiveness every time I have outbursts toward my children, and I will stop blaming them for my anger.

Are You Living with a Rose Bush Mom?

These guidelines are intended for spouses and children of Rose Bush moms. The best guidelines will come from the individualized Tall Trees Parenting Profile report, but these can help when a mom is a pure Rose Bush or a combination in which Rose Bush traits are dominant.

Perhaps you were raised by a mom who was a lot like Megan and a lot like me, also a Rose Bush: more of a disciplinarian than a nurturer. You may have suffered the same lack of gentle care that my daughter suffered and perhaps sometimes still does. You might experience lingering sadness or bitterness about this. Or perhaps you have forgiven your mom but still can't understand why things were so strained between you.

The Natural Rose Bush Mom, like any rose bush in nature, flourishes under certain conditions and becomes thorny in a different setting. If your Rose Bush mother knew herself well, she might have asked for things that helped her to flower more and prick less. As you read through the following points, seek to understand, accept, and forgive her as you discover that some of her needs were also perhaps unmet.

If you are the Rose Bush mom, stop pretending that you can cope with everything and admit:

I am most natural when
- You cooperate with me. A happy family is one in which everyone puts all their weight toward worthwhile goals.
- You entrust key decisions to me based on my experience and knowledge. When you question me about every decision, I feel that you doubt both my abilities and my love for you.

- You use clear words to make your needs known. I am bad at "sensing" them while living in the fast lane.

- You respond to my words and never ignore me. Even if your response is a negative one, I prefer it to the silent treatment.

- You let me be honest without assuming I'm being cruel. When I have to disguise my words, I feel false and deceitful. It's like I have two hearts: one that might hate when you do wrong and one that loves you endlessly.

- You let me do wild things occasionally that get my adrenaline pumping. I need to have a physical and mental rush at times.

- You give me a straight and honest opinion when I ask for one. If you can't bring yourself to say it, please write it down for me.

- You firmly and factually put me in my place when I deserve it. Superficial criticism or emotional pleading is easy for me to ignore, but when you set me right rationally, I will love you for it (after being a bit offended).

- You give me options and let me make the final choice. When you box me in with restrictions and demands, I become oppositional.

- You refrain from using a nagging or self-pitying approach to try to influence my decisions. I respond best to a calm and confident tone of voice.

- You believe that I love you very much even when I'm not in the mood to hug or kiss.

The Rose Bush Mom's First Step to (super)Natural Motherhood

Megan's parenting style clearly suits Kevin better than it suits Josh. Her way of doing things is not the only way, but she can't walk in two directions at once. She may reach a point with Josh where he is uncertain of her love just because she communicates it in a dialect so different from his own. Megan may need to consider making the following confessions to him someday.

All of us Rose Bush moms would do well to realize the same thing about our mothering style: we do have thorns and can't always retract them like a cat does its claws. The solution isn't to wish we weren't Rose Bushes. Our first step to (super)Natural Motherhood is simply to admit who we are and who we are not—to be real and transparent. If you are a Rose Bush, prayerfully ask God to show you which of these confessions you owe to your child or spouse:

I suspect you get hurt when
- I don't back out of a fight. I tend to see every discussion as a tug-of-war that only one of us can win.
- I sometimes forget that having your love is worth more than having you as an obedient subject.
- I become argumentative when you point out my mistakes. (Privately I may know I'm wrong; publicly I may vehemently deny it.)

- I misread your emotions or sometimes even ignore them because I am inept at dealing with intense feelings.
- I call things as I see them, without putting love above truth as I should when the truth is just my opinion and not God's Word.
- I say no easily, making it seem like I enjoy opposing you. I really don't.
- I always want to know the reasoning behind your decisions and won't stop questioning until I know you have thought about them. I can see how that would make you feel distrusted.
- I play only to win.
- I forget to let you be carefree and even careless every now and then.
- I am harsh and unfeeling. Half the time I don't notice this. Pray with me that God will give me greater sensitivity, as I don't mean to be mean.
- I call the shots about some things you are able to handle without my help and expect you to take control of some things you may not feel equipped for.
- I dismiss your opinions and interests in a way that makes you feel slow, stupid, and small.
- I violate the rules you make for certain situations simply because the rules seem arbitrary to me.

Most of all, I think I hurt you when I act as if you should change before you and I can be perfect for each other.

A Rose Bush Mom's Reflection of God's Heart

God has as His first agenda His own **honor**. We are created to reflect His glory. Only children who have been taught to honor—first their parents and, in so doing, God—will easily operate in the kingdom where God rules and we submit. Megan never allowed her children to treat her as if she's just a casual friend. They won't approach God without reverence either.

Obedience is an important key to the conditional promises of God. Some of His promises are unconditional, of course, but Megan is great at creating a consequential environment in which her children will learn that one can't claim rewards without having been obedient. If God asked Megan's children to go to the ends of the earth with no guarantee of safety or earthly reward, they would have had practice in being brave and obedient.

Megan puts emphasis on **commitment**. When she insists that her children continue with a task to the end, she is instilling in them an important trait that will make them extremely useful in the kingdom of God. They will be the ones who serve God even in the face of opposition. She sets the example by keeping her commitments too.

Trust is a key characteristic of faith. We can venture out in faith because we trust the character of God. Megan's children take risks because they recognize her trust in them. They also know her as a constant and **trustworthy** pillar of strength. Running to her as a refuge will train them to run to God.

Megan exhibits **fearlessness**. If her fearlessness can be grounded in the knowledge that He who is in her is greater than he who is in the world (1 John 4:4), instead of in the knowledge that she is tougher than most, she will give both her children a precious gift. A mother who stands this firmly on a revelation of the greatness of God teaches her children to do the same, even if they are naturally timid.

Megan loves Bible stories in which God is depicted as a **warrior**. She is one too. God has always fought for His children to the point where He annihilates their enemies. She gives her children the same security.

For Reflection

1. What do you like most about your temperament? Least?

2. Describe your ultimate goal in parenting. How will you measure the success of your efforts?

3. How do you balance law and grace in your home? Do you make accommodations for your children's temperaments?

4. What about parenting is most challenging or difficult for you? Do you ever ask for help with this difficulty?

5. Name three nondisciplinary ways in which you could nurture and show love to your children.

7

The (un)Natural Mom
of Pine Tree Place

Imagine yourself on a nature walk through a pine forest. It is cool, and the carpet of pine needles muffles most sounds. All you hear is the occasional snapping of a twig under your feet. You have the urge to spread a picnic blanket under the trees and linger a little. This is what people with a Pine Tree temperament are like: they are on a leisurely journey (or would like to be), are naturally unruffled, and have a calming effect on the rest of us. In a manner of speaking, Pine Trees have the calm of the forest inside them.

Once I wanted to uproot a small pine tree from the open field next to a nursery. I planned to display it during my seminars. The owner of the nursery had a good laugh when he saw my tiny plastic spade. He assured me that the roots were so deeply anchored that I would never be able to uproot even a small seedling with my inferior equipment. Pine Tree people are the same: strongly rooted, stubborn in a quiet way, and not eager to be transplanted.

Have you ever driven past a plantation of pine trees and called out, "Wow, look at that magnificent tree third from the left in row number five!" I'll bet you haven't, because one tends to see the collective greenery, not individual trees. In the same way, people with Pine Tree temperaments can go unnoticed, blending in with their surroundings. They don't advertise themselves and are perfectly happy to be in the background.

Just as pine trees are seldom found alone and are associated with Christmas celebrations and family gatherings, people with Pine Tree characteristics are attached to their nearest and dearest and are fond of tradition. Many of us grow up around a pine dining room table. The Pine Tree personality has the same desire to bring people together in a loving and peaceful circle. Even though they are not as outgoing as the Palm Trees in another neck of the woods, they love being with people just as much.

The Pine Tree temperament corresponds well with the phlegmatic temperament and also with the personality type S (supportive, steady, sincere) of the DiSC indicator. If you are familiar with these profiles, it will help you make sense of the mothering style of the Pine Tree mom.

A Day in the Life of Penny

Pine Tree mom Penny is only one example of a Pine Tree mom. Even if your test designated you as a Pine Tree, you will never identify with her in all respects. Don't let this bother you. Use her story as a guide, not a checklist. I happen to love Penny, as she represents the mom I want to be, but you might feel she is not your ideal role model. Look at her with mercy and get a feeling for the heart behind her mothering style. The same heart beats in you.

Penny is content and not at all keen to change just so you and I might like her better. I describe her as she was, is, and probably will be until her last day. God might deal with her in the same way He dealt with her biblical soul twin, Abraham: slowly and patiently.

Penny is forty-eight and married to Don, a Palm-Rose go-getter. They have a grown daughter, Sue, who is a newlywed, and a set of identical twins, Becky and Ruth, who are eight.

7:30 a.m. *In bed* Penny is awakened by her husband, who brought her a cup of coffee. It really helps. She drags herself up against the pillow until she's almost upright and finishes the coffee without opening her eyes. She can hear the reassuring sounds of the twins chatting in their room and Sue pouring milk over her cornflakes. Sue is visiting while her husband is out of town on business. Penny adores her family. She wishes it were Saturday so they could all stay in bed, read stories, and just be. And that it would rain so that they would have an excuse to eat pancakes. *Work, work, work* is the silly slogan of the world. How long will it take people to realize how pointless the rat race is? If everything could slow down just a tad … Her husband anxiously announces that she has ten minutes left to get ready. She can do it. She has easy hair and a simple makeup regime. She bathes in the evening to fall asleep more easily and to leave a short morning routine.

8:00 a.m. *In the car* She rushes back to the kitchen to grab a packet of caramel-flavored instant oatmeal—her favorite—and fills her travel mug with the second cup of coffee. She's almost fully awake now. She'll have the oats at the school. Sue seemed different this morning and wasn't saying much. Penny feels she can't leave home without giving her a hug. She waits for Sue to finish in the bathroom. She's running a little late by now, but this is important. Sue comes out of the bathroom, white as a sheet. Penny can't leave Sue like this, and she can't let down the twins, who have a class test first thing today, and she can't take leave either. Her mother hen instinct tells her to huddle. She helps Sue to the car, not sure what the plan is yet.

The twins are fighting. She shakes her head. *What can you do?* She lays down her one rule in a soft, steady voice: "If any of these words turns into violence, I'm making you wear the 'get-along shirt' again, okay?" The twins groan. The wide shirt has two neck holes and one sleeve on each side. They've been sentenced to the revolting restraint for offenses such as hair pulling, spitting, biting, pinching, and calling each other birdbrain. They stick to safe words but keep up the fight in the backseat. They're not strapped in. Penny is too distracted to notice. Sue really looks off-color. In spite of this, Penny is driving well below the speed limit.

8:15 a.m. *Outside the school* The twins dash out but are called back for compulsory kisses. Penny wishes them good luck with the test and tells them not to stress too much about it. Ruth should actually stress but doesn't; Becky stresses too much but needn't. "They're identical only on the outside," Penny says to Sue, who suddenly hurls herself forward and vomits into the coat on her lap. While putting a gentle hand on Sue's back and whispering "Ah, my girl, my sweet girl," Penny digs in her huge handbag and finds a hankie and a mint.

8:40 a.m. *At the high school where she works* Penny takes Sue to the nurse's office and soon has her cleaned up and smelling fresh. "Sue is married, isn't she?" the nurse asks. "I'm going to have to rule out pregnancy before I can give her anything."

"Oh, of course," is all Penny can think to say. She steps out into the hallway, processing. *Sue is just a baby. Her baby. She can't have a baby!*

She sees Samantha Jones, a sweet tenth grader, waiting at the little window of Penny's office. Samantha left her art portfolio at home. She asks if she can call her mom to bring it to school. Penny feels sorry for her. She regularly left important notes and books home at that age too. She helps the girl and promises to keep a lookout for her mom, Leanne. She knows all the parents. It makes her job easier because when you know them, you know where to be firm and where to make allowances.

The nurse calls her back but needs not say a word. The stunned expression on Sue's face says it all. Penny just holds her daughter and they cry a little. How grateful Penny is to be there for such a special moment. "You have to call Caleb right away. He's going to be a daddy!" Sue thinks he might not be thrilled. They're young and hadn't planned this. Penny reassures her. "He'll come around. You'll see."

9:30 a.m. *In the school's admin office* Penny brews them both a cup of ginger tea and finally prepares her packet of instant oats for breakfast. "This tea always settles an upset stomach, no matter what the cause," she assures Sue.

Penny leaves Sue only to take a few calls and send the most urgent emails. Every time someone steps into the office, she introduces her daughter without saying a word about the pregnancy. That's for Sue alone to share.

10:35 a.m. *Still in the office* Samantha's mom bursts in toting a large black folder. Penny can see that Leanne needs calming down. She comes out of the office and guides Leanne into a comfortable chair. Leanne gives her one look and starts letting it all out. Penny can't believe that this mom makes such a mountain out of a molehill. Her daughter really is a darling and all her concerns about Samantha are completely unfounded as far as Penny is concerned. Before she can even offer a word of comfort, Leanne leaps up, rattles off something Penny isn't quick enough to grasp, and speeds out the door.

10:50 a.m. *Back in the office* Penny's boss, the school principal, steps in and glances at Sue, puzzled. Penny ignores his expression and smiles. Unless he asks, she won't explain. He tells her three things he needs done immediately. Penny nods and gives the same answer as always: "I'll get right to it, sir." After he leaves, Penny takes a notepad out of her top drawer, thinks for a minute, then prioritizes her tasks.

She calls their neighbor to take Sue home to rest. Once Sue is safely picked up, Penny pours a second cup of tea and works steadily through her assignments until it's time to fetch the twins.

3:00 p.m. *At the school gate* Her eyes scan the swarm of schoolkids. She spots Becky first, who has a younger girl by the collar and a wild expression Penny has seen only once or twice before. Ruth gets involved next. She is grabbing at the girl's bag and pulling something out of it. A ring of spectators starts to form. Then a mom shoots past Penny's car on high heels, straight at the trio. She grabs each twin by the arm, yelling. That's enough to get Penny moving. She gets there as quickly as she can. It's chaos. Penny doesn't know who to pull away: the woman or the kids. Finally she gets out one feeble shriek: "Wait a minute!" Nobody even hears her above the commotion. She reaches in, takes hold of her two children, and pulls them toward her.

"So these brats are *yours?*" the victim's mom growls.

"They're my girls, yes. And you'll have to lower your voice or I'm going to need to leave."

"Bully girls with a coward for a mom!"

Penny won't be provoked. "I want to solve this as much as you do, Candice. There must have been a misunderstanding."

"How do you know my name?"

Penny has heard about Candice. She's known to wear a whole jewelry store on the fingers of one hand to hide the fact that she and her children recently lost everything they owned. If the rumors are true, her husband has filed for divorce. Penny has asked the moms who told her this to stop the gossip. She can see how hurt Candice is. She notices that the items everyone has been pulling on are a pair of ballerina shoes. "I remember you from ballet class," she fibs.

"Your daughters are stealing from my daughter! These are *hers*!" Candice nearly shoves the shoes in Penny's face.

Penny can clearly read the initials R. O. in her own handwriting inside Ruth's ballet shoes, and both twins are pointing and protesting. Penny looks at Candice with compassion and says, "I'm really sorry about their behavior. Please forgive us." Candice is turning red. She has just noticed the initials but has gone so far overboard that there is no way back to the ship. Penny just nods and takes her griping twins to the car without another word.

3:30 p.m. *At McDonald's* Penny pulls into the drive-through with two indignant eight-year-olds. She orders them each a Happy Meal with the healthiest options. They know what this is: comfort food. She parks in the shade, turns around in her seat, and smiles at the two, who are almost ready to forgive her. She is searching for the words. "Listen, the shoes we will replace before your next class, Ruth. But the behavior! When we get home, you are both making a 'sorry' card for that girl."

"But she stole my stuff and then said it was me, and then the crazy mom—"

"Wait, wait, wait. You never call an adult crazy. It's disrespectful, and I've told you before: crazy comes from a hurting place. Mrs. Candice, your friend's mom, is hurting, okay? And your friend is too."

"Why? What happened?"

Penny weighs her options before replying, "They've just had bad luck for a long time. It happens sometimes. They need to get lucky. That's why I let them win the fight. You girls are lucky already. Do you know why?"

"No."

"Because we are happy and healthy. We are all together and there is a wonderful surprise waiting at home."

"A puppy?"

"No. Something even better." While they're guessing the entire repertoire of legal and illegal pets between mouthfuls of burger and apple slices, Penny prays quietly for Candice's family.

4:15 p.m. *At home* Sue's morning sickness was kind enough to stop as soon as the morning was over. Sue has called Caleb and he was surprisingly happy about the news. Sue is sitting on the sofa waiting as the rest of the clan walk in.

"Where's the bearded dragon?" Becky calls into the living room, as if the pet would magically come forth and introduce itself. Instead, Sue whines, "I'm so tired of all the insults! I don't want children if they're going to be anything like you two!" She storms off in tears and slams the bedroom door.

Penny makes a motion in the direction of the twins, which they know to mean "Let it go" and walks to the slammed door. "Sweetie, I told the twins there was a surprise at home. They just guessed it was a dragon. They weren't talking about you. I just heard Dad's car pull up. You can tell everyone the good news when you're ready."

5:10 p.m. *In the kitchen* Penny has started making Sue's favorite meal. She's leaving out half the fat just in case it makes for another sick morning. She hasn't let anything slip yet but has a warm glow all over. She's going to be a grandma, and standing here cooking makes her feel all the readier for the role. She completely forgets about the notes of apology the twins were supposed to write. She's in a different place now.

6:30 p.m. *In the living room* Sue finally joins them, and everyone sits comfortably around the room with their plates on trays. The twins are on the carpet. Stains are proof that this is their default dining space. When Sue was younger, Penny was strict about eating at the table but gave up when it became too much of a nag with the twins.

Don gives a fast-paced account of his entire eventful day, and Penny beams back pride and gratitude. He has achieved so much in life. She feels lucky about that as well. Sue's mood has improved considerably. Penny's culinary skills are to be credited for that. "Caleb and I are having a baby!" Sue exclaims and jumps into her dad's arms as she's done since she was a little girl. Afterward he leans over and gives Penny a drawn-out kiss. She responds by holding his face in both hands and saying with affection that could never be mistaken for an insult: "I love you, Grandpa!"

They spend the rest of the evening paging through Sue's baby albums and rehashing stories. Penny hasn't felt happier in years.

She notices that the twins have fallen asleep on the floor. She reminisces about their baby days as she carries them one by one to their beds. The rocking chair she had made especially for feeding both of them at once is still in the corner of the room. She curls up on it and watches their angelic faces until she is sure they're out for the count. At least Becky, but perhaps Ruth as well, was only pretending to sleep through the process of being carried up to bed. They were avoiding having to brush their teeth. She knows the game. Tomorrow is another day. Teeth won't rot in one night. This is a special night.

Don is in bed, reading the news on his tablet. She snuggles up to him, puts her head on his soft belly, and drifts off without setting her alarm clock.

Pine Tree through the Seasons of Motherhood

Penny finds solace at her favorite table in her favorite coffee shop, where she has half a portion of carrot cake and a cup of Earl Grey tea every Wednesday. It's been like that for almost twenty-five years. The owner of The Lemon Orchard loves Penny dearly, though they've never had a heart-to-heart conversation in all these years. Penny's table is right next to the owner's tiny office, and through the thin walls she has had the honor of hearing the wisdom, struggles, and joys Penny shares with her closest friends. She remembers snippets of these conversations because of the sincerity and warmth in Penny's words, which often came at just the right time for her too.

Deciding to Start a Family

Penny had a small bridal shower here at The Lemon Orchard. There were about ten women, who all clearly cared about her. She seems the type who has fewer but deeper friendships. There was the customary joking around about frilly underwear and honeymoon tips, and she had to pass a quiz about family planning. I heard her say, "I'm not too worried about that, really. Babies come when it's their time, and I'm ready to be a mom."

Pregnancy

Not a month after her honeymoon, as I recall, she came in looking the same as she always does but ready to break the news that she was pregnant. Penny has always been steady and serene. You'd think she'd laugh and giggle and do a surprise reveal by showing up with a bib or something—I've seen some crazy things!—but she just invited three friends for tea and said after about half an hour of listening to her friends talk about their lives, "We are already expecting."

In the following months, she still came, often skipping the carrot cake. She cared a lot about the health of the baby. She allowed herself a decaf cappuccino every now and then, though. She kept seeing her friends regularly, and I noticed she talked about babies with the ones who had kids but not with the ones who were struggling to get pregnant. She was extremely thoughtful that way.

About two years later, Penny and her husband decided to start on baby number two, but it just wasn't working. I heard her so many times talking about this longing but never blaming or questioning God or the doctors or anything at all. She often said, "But then again, we don't know what's best for us, do we?" or, "I still have time." As I recall, it took twelve years before they finally had the twins!

Baby Days

She was so happy and easygoing as a mom, even with the twins. I can still see her waddling in with a baby carrier in each hand and a bulging diaper bag over her shoulder. That bag was like a magician's hat: anything and everything those babies needed was in there. She always had a blanket to spread between her chair and the wall, where she'd set out all sorts of baby toys to keep the twins occupied.

Sometimes she'd feed them right then and there—discreetly, of course, but still to the surprise and even offense of some of my customers. I recall a yuppie once said, "This is hardly the place—!" And Penny completed her sentence: "—to be eating and drinking? I thought that's what we all do here."

She clearly loved having her babies with her. If they were too difficult, she'd just apologize, scoop them up, and say something like "Guess someone needs a nap! Let's continue our visit at my house."

Toddler Training

Penny was never clean during the twins' toddler years. She allowed them to feed her sweets from sticky hands, climb on her lap with muddy feet, and wipe their noses on her dress. It was like she had turned into a canvas and welcomed the life her kids were painting onto it. I thought we should all be more like that.

Penny was firm with her first child, Sue. She tried to do things by the book but really didn't seem in her element as that kind of mother. You could tell she doubted herself: *Should I be strict now? What should I do? I hope this works and people don't think I'm mean.*

I never saw Penny insist that the twins do something they didn't want to. If they ever complained, she'd find an alternative. If she had ordered a snack they didn't like, for instance, she'd let them pick something else. She wasn't spoiling them as much as she was keeping the peace.

Penny had a little bit more patience with the twins than I would have had. She let them nag for something on and on without saying either a firm no or a clear yes. One could tell she wanted to say no but also avoid full-scale waterworks. That led to an explosion of tempers more than once.

I think she did want her kids to be well behaved, but she may have underestimated how much energy it would take to discipline them consistently. If she'd ever flown out of her chair, I'd have assumed that the coffee shop was on fire. Nothing got her to jump up! With toddlers, that is a skill you need. I wish she had it that day when one twin decided to try out the curtain for a swing. Penny just slowly raised her arms, dropped her jaw, and froze as we all witnessed the gleeful scream and the entire pelmet and curtains come off the wall to bury that tot in yards and yards of thick curtaining. Even then she didn't move. I was there first to dig out the kid. All Penny said was, "Thank goodness the rod didn't come down on her head!"

In the heat of the moment, she couldn't think straight. It was as if she had to process it to reach the conclusion that she should make amends. Upon her return the next week, she apologized profusely and insisted on paying for the damages.

School Years

Penny was not as excited as most moms whose youngest has started school. She did take those first-day-of-school pictures and showed them to her friends, but as she sat here with those pictures, she looked as though she might cry, which in Penny terms meant she was cut up and bleeding inside. She always fetched her oldest from school. She didn't want other moms to do it.

She complained a little about the early mornings and how the school took up so much of their family time. She didn't enjoy sports on Saturdays. In her mind, it didn't leave the kids enough time to just play and be carefree. I don't think she served on a single school committee. She had a phobia of fund-raisers. She said she just couldn't ask strangers for money. She avoided serving at the refreshment stands, saying, "Am I the only person who can't calculate correct change under pressure?"

She never bought into the achievement culture around her either. She never showed off pictures of her kids getting awards or participating in the school play like other moms often did.

Her kids didn't have perfect attendance records. About once a year she kept them home from school if they were especially sad or stressed. I remember this because I thought it was profound of her to realize that sometimes a broken heart is a better reason to take a day off than a fever. She seemed like a mother hen to me, forever gathering the chicks under her wings.

Parenting Teens

Penny came to The Lemon Orchard a lot while her oldest was a teen. She ate slowly and sometimes didn't finish her tea. She listened to her friends more and spoke even less. I knew the signs: she clearly was worried about her daughter's behavior. The child was rebellious and rude to her mother. Penny didn't deserve it, but then again she seldom insisted on being addressed with respect. She had allowed that girl to be rude, if you ask me, and opened herself up to hurtful verbal attacks. Her friends gave disciplinary advice, but Penny wanted to fix the relationship, not the behavior. She said such things as "I don't want her to mind me because she doesn't want to lose her cell phone for a week; I want her to mind me because she loves me for a lifetime." She sounded like a Hallmark card, yet she was so sincere that I felt every word.

When her oldest was around sixteen, Penny didn't come in for a month or more. I overheard two of her friends say she had been admitted to a clinic for stress. I could hardly believe it. She never seemed stressed. I heard her best friend say that Penny had many fears and regrets. Sue had become sexually active, and when Penny found out, she was devastated. Talking about sex was something she couldn't bring herself to do. She had given her daughter a book but never made sure Sue was really informed. The psychologist felt Penny needed to learn to be a lot more proactive and deal with confrontation and conflict. According to the friend, when Penny had her first session, she had to name three characteristics of her husband that she disliked. She simply couldn't. She never learned to allow herself to be honest in that way. If she admitted there were problems, she would have to deal with them. She didn't want to, so denying them worked better for her.

It is happening all over again with the twins now. She is worried about them but never speaks about her concerns. They have slight learning disabilities she never dealt with. She hopes they will just outgrow them, but not all the problems can be easily remedied, from what I hear. I just hope she will face these things before the twins are teens. I'd hate to see her in that desperate state again.

Letting Go

Well, clearly this is hard for Penny. She never worked while the oldest was in school. If I remember correctly, she started working at the high school when the twins were seven. She's still close to them that way, as the high school is just across the street from their elementary school. Her grown daughter also spends a lot of time at Penny's house. I think Penny would not mind if Sue and her son-in-law moved in with them.

Penny lets go of things easily but not of people. I saw her lose a purse, an earring she inherited from her grandmother, and many baby items over the years. It never phased her, but to this day she orders the spinach and feta quiche every August 4. It's the anniversary of her mom's death. Her mom loved the quiche. She's almost celebrating it. I think it's a way of holding on.

"Granny Pine" Years

She's more of a granny than a mom already. So kind—so spoiling and doting. I can imagine other people's kids calling her Nana. She just has that homeliness you can't miss. I can see her knitting baby booties, baking cookies, and reading stories to the grandkids at bedtime. I bet she smells of cinnamon and apple pie over the holidays.

The Natural Pine Tree Mom

We almost had to dig to find anything unnatural about Penny, didn't we? Pine Tree moms often fit the stereotype of the Natural Mom. But even they have their days when they have to admit to unnaturalness. It is usually the strict and stern aspects of motherhood and the need to be actively involved that they have difficulty with.

I find their eagle-eyed view of life to be their best natural gift. You'll have to go far to find a Pine Tree mom who loses her long-term perspective or gets caught up in silly things. I suspect that actress and blogger Mayim Bialik is a Pine Tree. I found many pine tree needles scattered among her blog: "Don't listen to anyone's advice. Listen to your baby.... There are so many books, doctors, and well-meaning friends and family. We like to say, 'You don't need a book. Your baby is a book. Just pick it up and read it.'"[1]

Sometimes Pine Tree moms are dealt the seemingly ill-fitting hand to be the mother of a child who is her exact opposite: feisty, dramatic, on the stage, out there, and loud. Here's what two such women have to say about their mothers, who both sound like Pine Trees to me:

My mother is everything to me. She's my anchor; she's the person I go to when I need to talk to someone. She is an amazing woman.
Demi Lovato

There were times when, in middle school and junior high, I didn't have a lot of friends. But my mom was always my friend. Always.
Taylor Swift

It often seems to me as if Pine Tree moms sacrifice themselves on the altar of motherhood and reap the reward of children who rise higher than they ever rose. Unfortunately, I have also seen these mothers' hearts ripped out by children who aren't nearly appreciative enough of this grand gift.

The Pine Tree Mom and Nurturing

What Becky says: She always has time for a hug, and she never lets go first. I think she would hold us all day long if she could! That's why she has soft arms.

We learned in school that orangutans build a new nest for their babies every single night and nurse them until they're six or seven, always carrying them. I thought of my mom. She's like that.

What Sue says: I have a lot of warm memories about being in her arms, on her lap, sleeping or just sitting next to her. She sometimes bribed us to rub her back and shoulders or play with her hair.

Mom is a mood fixer. When you're out of sorts, she'll be the first to notice and do something that will help. She was especially caring during finals week and saw to it that I took regular breaks and never went into an exam with junk food in my system.

What her husband says: She sat up with our kids so many nights. If they had the slightest fever, she'd make a complete bed for them right next to ours, move into their rooms with a whole pharmacy of goodies, or pop the little ones into bed with us. There were times when I wished I were a baby again because one clearly got the most love by being sick, crying, or appearing helpless.

I'll admit I've been jealous a few times when I see her and the kids chat for hours about little secrets I will never know anything about. I don't think they were ever afraid or ashamed to tell her their thoughts and feelings.

Penny's superpower is caring. In between having our babies, she cared for so many stray and injured animals that our home often looked and smelled like an animal clinic.

Many children in our neighborhood and at church will tell you she's their "other mother." You should see her with the kids at the school where she works. The sick ones go to her for comfort before going to the nurse, and the ones disciplined by the principal get their consolation hug from "Mrs. Penny" before returning to class.

The Pine Tree Mom and Discipline

What her husband says: She tries to keep order but does it with gentle words rather than a firm grip. She aggravates nothing. She doesn't usually get to the bottom of the issue, but she definitely calms down the emotions around it. When the kids were little, she'd just distract, redirect, or remove them from the situation in which they were misbehaving. She feels that many parents escalate the situation by disciplining kids in the moment. She believes that children won't misbehave when they are fed, secure, happy, and healthy. So when they do misbehave, she'll feed them, love on them, cheer them up, make sure they aren't cold or hot, see to it that they're feeling well, and take them to a happier place.

What Ruth says: When I break or lose something, I tell Mom before Dad finds out because then she forgives and forgets to tell him what I did. She even feels sorry for me when I mess up and cry about it.

When you don't do what Mom asks, she'll get quiet and sad. She'll tell you how it makes her feel or she'll just walk away. That's how you know it's trouble. She'll tell Dad, and he'll get on your case for her.

Our mom gets mean only when we are mean to one another. It doesn't bother her too much if you make a mess in your room or get not-so-great marks on your school project. But if you do something mean to someone, she gets mad. Then she feels bad about getting mad and tries to make everything okay again.

What Sue says: Mom definitely is way too lenient with the twins. They can do what they want. She never believes that what they do is on purpose. She thinks that everyone always does their best and that when they do badly, one shouldn't be harsh. It's kind to look at people like that, but the twins take advantage of her kindness.

The Pine Tree Mom and Training

What Sue says: Mom loved doing things with me growing up: cooking, cleaning, gardening, shopping, watching movies. She never made me work too hard. As soon as I got a little tired, she announced a snack break.

Sometimes I want to get better at doing things, but she doesn't tell me what I do wrong. Once I made really flat cinnamon buns and wanted to know what went wrong. She kept saying they were fine even though they clearly weren't. She felt too sorry for me to come right out and say what I did wrong. I had to ask my dad, who immediately said it was the leavening. I had no idea what that was, so I asked Mom. She took me to the dry-yeast packets and gently asked if the water had been warm enough to activate the yeast. I had used cold water. My mom still ate at least three or four of those dry buns.

What Becky says: Mom lets us try things even when we make a mess. She likes it when we keep ourselves busy so that she can relax a bit. When we struggle and get frustrated, she doesn't always feel like figuring it out with us. She'll say, "Honey, if it's too hard, just leave it. We'll try again when you're a little taller, okay?" She says "taller" because she doesn't want to make us angry by saying we're small.

The Pine Tree Mom and Coping with Life in General

What other moms say: Notes don't often make it back to school on time. She won't ever die of a heart attack, that's for sure. She has this inborn "Tomorrow is another day" approach to life. We start gathering school supplies for projects a month in advance. The day before school starts, she'll call one of us asking where to buy the supplies and whether one of us perhaps still has the list. She probably leaves all the letters, lists, and bills in a drawer, where they lie gathering urgency till heaven knows when.

To me she's the Natural Mom, baking goodies, packing treats for camping, never fussing about messy beds or wet floors. She just has too much grace to turn anything into a strict program. She may have tried reward charts a few times, but I get the impression she dislikes keeping track of mistakes.

I think she sees only her children's hearts and not their appearances or achievements. She doesn't try to make them seem better than they are or do better than they are doing. She is so content. I wish I could be like that with my kids!

What Sue says: With Mom, what you see is what you get. She is the same at home, at church, and at work.

It's as though unhappiness in the home paralyzes her. Whenever any of us went through something tough, she also went through it, even if we didn't talk about it.

Mom sort of lives her life around our lives. She has only one hobby: gardening, and the rest of the time she just tries to be a good mom and a good wife. I think she can hardly remember the dreams she had as a young girl. If any of us would go and live far away, she would feel empty.

What Ruth says: Mom definitely likes being home more than being at work. She could sit and just watch us play and be happy. The only thing that stresses her out is when she and dad have a fight. She gets all quiet and weird. She can't think straight and forgets things. Once they make peace, she's normal again.

What her husband says: Penny always strives to make our house a home. She loves to create comfortable surroundings. There is a garden bench for two, where she likes to take me for a chat, and a bay window with pillows, where she likes to read the kids stories.

Our physical well-being is central to her. She is an earth mother who grows her own greens and brews special teas for our ailments and stress. She prompts me to get more exercise and fresh air. I'm sure she wants me to outlive her. She can't stand the idea of loneliness, even though she needs time to herself.

Penny is as steady as a rock. The kids and I see her as an island in rough waters. We cling to her. But she's hard to read, even after all these years. I think she's had some tough times with the twins especially, but you have to ask; otherwise you wouldn't know.

Are You a Pine Tree Mom?

In Penny, you've seen the positive impact you make on the people around you in your unassuming way. If you've obtained your individualized Tall Trees Parenting Profile (T^2P^2), you will have seen your unique list of parenting strengths:

- I am nurturing.
- I am a peacemaker.
- I think before I act or speak.
- I put family above my own ambitions.
- I have a calming effect on my household.
- I always strive to create harmony in the home.
- I am not demanding or forceful with my children.
- I am a safe place where my family can start over after failures.

- I know what the important issues are and don't sweat the small stuff.

Even though you effortlessly avoid the mistakes of feistier types, you, like Penny, have areas in which you can grow. The T²P² report contains your personalized growth plan. The key growth areas for those with dominant Pine Tree parenting traits are fairly similar, so the following suggestions will likely make sense to you. You might resist working off a list like this one, but how will you work on relationships unless you do so intentionally? If you struggle to change in these areas, remember that God is the One who effects all change in us. Ask Him to do it and to make you willing to change as you practice these commitments:

- I'll stand up for my spouse and children, even if it will likely cause conflict.
- I won't let my love of comfort and stability cause myself or my family to miss an adventure.
- I'll learn to speak about what's in my heart so my family can know me more deeply.
- I won't keep my wisdom to myself but will invest it in the next generation.
- I won't sweep unhappiness under the rug; I'll sort it out.
- I'll take an active role in shaping my children's behavior, the sooner the better.
- When I see issues that need attention, I'll take initiative instead of waiting for others to do so.

Are You Living with a Pine Tree Mom?

All of us would be more comfortable if those closest to us were just like us, wouldn't we? It just so happens that God seems to be more interested in our maturity than in our comfort. If the Pine Tree mom in your life stretches you beyond your comfort zone, be assured that you do the same to her. Being the utmost creature of comfort, she likely feels more unease than you do. Have you ever seen a plant growing where the wind is too strong for it? It grows crooked and remains bent even when the wind dies down. Pine Trees can easily be pushed over by continuous resistance. The everyday challenges of parenting and life may have done this to your Pine Tree mom or Pine Tree wife. There are ways to show compassion to her and to shelter her from life's winds. This is how she might ask for help if it weren't so hard for her to acknowledge her own needs:

You show me love when

- You let me smother and mother you. TLC won't kill you, and I don't do it because I think you're a baby; I do it because we won't always have each other.
- You help me say no so that I don't become a people pleaser. I feel terrible when I say no, but you can remind me that I always have a choice and need not be the victim of people with more forceful personalities than mine.
- You give me time with just you. Group time means little to me compared to one-on-one time. I open up my heart only in the safety of your focused attention.

- You think about your contribution to a problem even after I have apologized for mine, as I'm not necessarily admitting guilt. Apologizing is often just my way of ending the fight.
- You let me think carefully before expecting a final answer. Under pressure I will say what I think you want to hear or become stubborn and stuck as a defense mechanism. Then you'll never know what I really wanted.
- You lovingly encourage me without any insult. I rise to your gentle suggestions but shut down under hurtful words.
- You have grace with my slower pace. I will get where I need to be in a much better mood than when I'm pushed or pulled.
- You allow me to withdraw from situations that are too loud, busy, dangerous, or competitive. I can enjoy these situations more as a spectator than as a participant.
- You give me security by building traditions and stability with me. This means putting up with things that may have become boring to you but have become my "happy place," and putting up with the same people again and again: my safety net.
- You allow me plenty of time to relax without thinking I'm lazy. I may not seem to be a hard worker, but a lot goes on that you don't see and that I don't brag about.

- You help me express my feelings without asking a lot of questions. I speak my heart when I feel safe with you. I'm like an oyster. I'll roll out pearls for you once I'm ready to open up. It will be worth your while.
- You join in my striving for peace in our home. Some fights can be fought without screaming. Some issues can be dealt with when everyone is calm. Some issues can be left alone entirely. Trust me.
- You talk less about "you" and "me" and more about "us" so that I know we're always on the same side. I may spend quite a bit of time by myself, but I'm always part of the team.
- You give me credit for my good intentions, not just for results. My attitude is often much better than my performance.
- You help me break down huge tasks into smaller chunks so that I don't feel overwhelmed. I'm not the Energizer Bunny, and challenges don't excite me. I need to know that things are achievable before I set out to achieve them bit by bit.

Encourage your Pine Tree mom (or any mom who has a combination type with large proportions of Pine Tree) to complete a Tall Trees Parenting Profile. The profile will speak for her when she is reluctant to complain or make demands. Instead of being frustrated with how distant or quiet she can be and how hard it is to know what she is thinking and feeling, you can use this profile report to get to know her in order to love her better. She deserves it.

The Pine Tree Mom's First Step to (super)Natural Motherhood

You may know from experience that your parenting style works better for some of your kids than for the others. Likewise, some phases are more challenging than others, aren't they? Like Penny, you may have had tough years with a teen or even a grown child.

Although you are not the ultimate speech master, there may come a day when you want to acknowledge the items on the following list to one or all of your children and even to your spouse. Doing that will be your first step to (super)Natural Motherhood. If it's too confrontational to say these things face-to-face, showing the list to loved ones could take your relationship to a deeper level. It can help them realize that you never intentionally did them harm or neglected their needs out of spite; you were simply being a Natural Pine Tree Mom. Sometimes we have to apologize even when the effects of our actions are unintentional or when we failed to do something that could have been helpful. Forgiveness is not just letting go of a painful incident; it's also letting go of the unrealistic expectations another person cannot meet. If your family members feel let down in any way, you can use these words to help them forgive you:

Forgive me for disappointing you when
- I sometimes don't want to say or show how I feel. Emotions are easier to handle when they're yours than when they're mine.
- I procrastinate until the last possible moment, especially when the work looks involved. I realize this has implications for your life.

- I watch as you do your thing instead of joining in.
- I give you the silent treatment when I'm hurt. I'd rather say nothing than hurt you back. I feel like I'm in a catch-22 because when I say nothing, that hurts you too.
- I forget a lot of the details and specifics of the things you tell me because to me only the core matters. I want to attend to the details that matter to you, but I seem to lack that kind of wiring.
- I avoid places where I can be put on the spot and sometimes keep you away from those as well, forgetting that you may be more able to handle the spotlight than I am.
- I move on when bad things happen and try not to go backward, even when you need to go back to sort things out.
- I refuse to argue with you. I can tell you lose respect for me when I back off.
- I freeze and withdraw when you scream. I want to learn to be able to handle intense emotion.
- I cut people out of our lives who are quick to get angry, rude, or forceful, even when they are your good friends or family.
- I stay uninvolved when I think something is none of my business, when you do in fact need me to step in.
- I set lower goals and standards for myself than what you have for me.
- I take a lot of breaks, need a lot of rest, and can't be as energetic as you.

- I struggle with self-motivation. Sometimes I need you to nudge me a little. I can see that I'm a drag then.
- I don't like leaving my comfort zone. Perhaps we can start with short trips beyond my borders?
- I can be possessive and overprotective of you and sometimes even hog your time. I give you permission to tell me when you feel smothered.
- I avoid taking the lead or responsibility for fear of letting someone down.

Most of all: forgive me for forgetting that God's perfect plan for us can include uncomfortable growth in each of us.

A Pine Tree Mom's Reflection of God's Heart

Penny epitomizes **peace**. One of the names of God is "Prince of Peace" (Isa. 9:6 NIV), and peacemakers have the promise in the Beatitudes that "they will be called children of God" (Matt. 5:9 NIV). We are called to strive for peace in relationships. Penny's children will have a prime example in their mom's dealings with people.

Contentment is often a by-product of peace. Isn't it discontent that drives so many of our peace-destroying actions and words? Penny models a serene acceptance of the hard and the happy moments alike. She embraces how things are rather than building fantastic dreams about how things could be. Instead of harboring regrets, she lives in the present moment. This "light" living is the life of resting in Christ (Heb. 4:10), which anyone can choose but many don't.

When God revealed Himself to Moses, He said that He is "the **compassionate** and **gracious** God, **slow to anger, abounding in love** and **faithfulness**" (Exod. 34:6 NIV). Penny's children are more likely to believe this than are children raised in a home where their every mistake is punished harshly. Pine Tree moms have an advantage: they are not as explosive as the more emotional tree types. They have a bomb inside them with an unnaturally long fuse. This patience creates a safe place to grow.

Penny's **faithfulness** in praying for her children will probably create life circumstances that teach them what she has left untaught. Thus, her faithfulness may look different from the faithfulness of the workhorses among us. Hers will be rooted in a single-minded trust in God.

Penny's **self-control** when it comes to her tongue is a wonderful asset (James 3:2). She thinks before she speaks. There may be more verses in Proverbs about the wisdom of **careful speech** than about any other virtue. Penny and most other Pine Tree moms have this self-control. If she keeps the balance by speaking up bravely when she must speak up, she will have taught her children one of the most important relational skills one can ever learn.

Jesus, even though He is a king, rode into the city of Jerusalem on a donkey and proceeded to serve His disciples by washing their feet, feeding them bread, and offering them wine (John 12–13). Penny serves with exactly these practical acts of **humility**, which teach her children the most vital characteristic of true leadership: **selfless service**.

For Reflection

1. How close is your personality to Penny's? What do you admire about her?

2. What are your favorite resources for parenting wisdom? Which do you tend to avoid? Why?

3. When you can't "fix" a problem going on in your home with your children or spouse, how do you cope with feelings of powerlessness?

4. Which aspect of your present parenting season feels like a mismatch with the Pine Tree mothering style? Which tree type would you think could handle it with ease?

5. Name one risk you can take to improve your relationship with your children.

8

The (un)Natural Moms from Elsewhere

Have you read the previous chapters without a clear aha feeling of seeing yourself in Leanne, Jessica, Megan, or Penny? Perhaps you are among the roughly 60 percent of mothers who have a combination personality of two tree types.

Even though your own Tall Trees Parenting Profile will surely help you see yourself more clearly, I would like to give you a portrait of some of these combination moms. As you read through these, please consider Jesus's teaching: "Each tree is recognized by its own fruit. People do not pick figs from thornbushes, or grapes from briers" (Luke 6:44 NIV). Marvel at the wonder of these (un)Natural Moms with their wonderfully natural designs. Make space in your heart for them. It is easy for misunderstandings, suspicions, and offenses to creep between people who have such different approaches to parenting. It is my hope that these profiles will broaden every mother's appreciation for each other. Perhaps you can take a pencil and write the names of mothers you know next to the categories they fit as a first step to learning to love them better.

Use the results of your free Tall Trees Parenting Profile to determine which of these (un)Natural Moms has the most in common with you.

The (un)Natural Mom on Box-Rose Hill

Together Megan and Leanne can accomplish a mountain of tasks, only to feel that there is still so much more to do and it should have been done yesterday. This is a concise summary of the Box-Rose mom, who is effective, productive, hardworking, and often a slave to perfectionism and striving. I know this mom the best, because I am her. The slightly nervous and overwhelmed Leanne combined with the confident achiever Megan seems like a superwoman to outsiders. Her inner turmoil and tension would surprise other moms. Box-Roses seem in control even when shaking in their high-heel boots. They don't keep it all together without sacrificing a whole lot of rest, health, peace, and reflection time. "Do, do, do instead of be, be, be leads to a lot of me, me, me." Yes, I know it's a tacky cliché, but the Box-Roses will understand. We tend to be constantly busy with ourselves and our challenges.

Box-Rose moms make up a core group in the committees that execute the school and church plans. They source, inspect, organize, and pay the team uniform manufacturers. They compile the protest documentation when an inappropriate book is assigned to their sixth graders. They make sure the church camp is a success. They are front dogs in the sleigh team, so to speak.

At home they want acknowledgment for how hard they work, but that does not always score points with the child who is sunburned, hungry, heartbroken, or bullied at school. This child needs the Box-Rose mom to unbuckle her tool belt and lay aside the wooden spoon or laptop to listen to a hurting heart. "Oh please!" sigh the Box-Roses in one chorus, as their capacity for personal problems is a lot lower than their capacity for practical problem solving.

They can sort out the bully, slap on the aloe vera lotion, whip up a snack, and paint the big picture about love as long as they don't have to get mushy about it.

The Box-Rose mom also
- Is serious about her work and fights the things that interfere or interrupt (sometimes even her family).
- Is not fond of joking around or playing childish games.
- Has X-ray vision that can spot mistakes. To you they are hidden; to her they are obvious.
- Tends to compare herself with other moms and her children with other moms' children.
- Becomes impatient or judgmental when others don't see a situation the way she does.
- Takes criticism personally. (Give it anyway or she will never know where she can grow.)
- Avoids cuddling and smooching, especially when she's a little stressed.
- Defends her territory because she keeps her own kind of order there.
- Will work herself to a standstill to meet a deadline and your needs.
- Doesn't need people as much as others do and can go away without missing you every second of every day.
- Can find it hard to forgive and forget, because she likes justice so much.

To express love to a Box-Rose,

- Tell her you are proud of her achievements as a mother and woman outside your home. She always has a lingering insecurity that needs to be put to rest, no matter how confident she seems.
- Trust her and tell her that you do. There is no end to the effort she will put in to prove that your trust was not misplaced.
- Help her find a fresh challenge after each completed task. In the no-man's-land between goals, she can become depressed and might take it out on you.
- Support her while she's working on a long-term project. The best support is to take other duties off her hands so that she can focus and finish well.
- Allow her to try to correct mistakes: her own and yours. She's a problem solver and doesn't want you to sweep anything under the rug.
- Remind her to celebrate a job well done before diving into the next task. She needs to learn to enjoy the fruit of hard work, and you may be just the one to share in the feast.
- Give her the right to make decisions, knowing she is not impulsive but thorough. She'll respond in kind when the decision is one she knows you're better suited to make.
- Volunteer to be her helper, and assist her eagerly. She almost needs a clone. The closer you can copy her own efforts, the better.

- Offer her a tried-and-tested plan when she is stuck. Give it to her in writing because she will first tear it down and then extract what she can use. It gets messy. Step back.
- Pray for her as she struggles to come to terms with disappointment instead of trying to cheer her up. She can be helped only from the inside.
- Respect that her body can love you only when her heart and mind have come to rest. Your password: "What can I do to make your life easier today?" Often she just needs an invitation to vent about the day.

To help her be natural,
- Allow her to work where she chooses and in a way that works for her.
- Save the chatting and touching for when she is finished with her tasks.
- Accept her need to feel effective and productive, so let her finish things she starts.
- Let her attend events where she can learn from highly skilled and knowledgeable people.
- Tell her exactly what you need and when so she can fit it into her schedule.
- Don't make things easier unless she asks you to.
- Let her work long hours as long as she keeps a balance and does not harm her health.
- Encourage her to improve all the time, even when you think she is already good enough, but focus on character more than on work.

- Give her important tasks to do. She wants responsibility, not mundane jobs.
- Have high expectations of her; she tends to live up to them.

The (un)Natural Mom in Pine-Palm Woods

The Pine-Palm mom seems amazingly natural to those who comprise the task-oriented tree types. Palms squeeze people and cheer them on; Pines hug and serve them. Imagine having a mixture of cheerleader Jessica and mother-hen Penny as a mom! Neither gets stuck in the negatives, and neither is known for her demands and high standards. They seem to create a valley of green grass and cool waters for others wherever they go. (If I seem biased, I probably am just in awe of them. I am better at creating boot camps than pastures of pleasure and rest.)

Peace and joy are Pine-Palm moms' highest goals. They will embrace parenting advice that doesn't require them to confront or correct their children, because stern discipline and the pursuit of harmony don't seem to mesh. They prefer approaches that assure them of love's power and support their belief that children can outgrow their sinful nature without painful pruning.

Their families may suffer a bit under their failures to budget, manage time, and keep up with demanding schedules. They live for the moment. Planning ahead seems silly to them because they've seen how life tends to wipe out plans regardless of how far in advance they are made.

They find fulfillment primarily in relationships and are the most likely combination to find complete gratification in motherhood. They have no pressing need to achieve in the corporate world. Only work that builds community, serves people, brings joy, and improves lives will motivate them to sacrifice time with their families in favor of a career.

The Pine-Palm mom is a beautiful creature who tends to mother not just her own children but also the children of others.

The Pine-Palm mom also
- Avoids taking full responsibility for failure. She tends to expect people to look at her heart and excuse her "sins of omission."
- Rolls with the punches of life in a way that helps her children to move on too.
- Deals badly with sadness and stress. She tends to go into denial or escape mode.
- Can't follow logic when her emotions are strong, because her heart overrules her head.
- Will do more favors than one can reasonably ask of her just to be loved and accepted.
- Forgives and forgets easily, except when her nearest and dearest are harmed.
- Can celebrate anyone's victories, not only her family members'.
- Believes that tomorrow is another day and parenting is not a race.
- Tends to be happy and satisfied with her life more often than not.
- Gives encouragement and compliments freely and sincerely.

- More or less likes all people (except the really rude ones).
- Loves people more than activities and material things.
- Is moved by the needs and emotions of others.
- Is a giver of time, space, grace, and kind words.
- Is easy to live with.

To express love to a Pine-Palm,
- Encourage her to serve using her specific gifts. Happiness and harmony are her superpowers, and she'll wilt away if she can't use them.
- Spend quality "fun time" with her, and tell her how she makes you happy and why you genuinely like her.
- Let her tackle one tough thing at a time instead of weighing her down with multiple goals at once.
- Admire her heart, not just her housework and achievements. Being is more important to her than doing. Measure her by this standard.
- Allow her to be fulfilled rather than ambitious and to be content rather than competitive.
- Comfort her with a favorite snack or activity every now and again. Her batteries need recharging after every demanding parenting effort.
- Give her girl time with her closest friends. You will reap the benefits of a really happy mom.
- Allow her to follow her heart rather than a program. The people who write the parenting books are rarely like her. Their regimes choke her.

- Protect her from unkind people and fight some battles for her. She makes love, not war, but sometimes the battle comes right to her doorstep of its own accord.
- Touch her with care when she's tired and with passion when she's not. Use your imagination.
- Allow her to change her mind instead of toughing it out through poor decisions. When the joy is gone, it's gone. She's unable to function without joy.

To help her be natural,
- Allow her to figure things out as she goes along instead of having things mapped out in advance.
- Don't expect her to remember a flood of words. Be ready to repeat, remind, and restart!
- Let her talk through things with you until she understands the intention behind your words.
- Include her in your relationships and socials. She can't be happy standing outside looking in.
- Assist her with planning and schedules for the household if you're better at it than she is.
- Make it about relationship when you explain why things are important to you.
- Don't expect her to walk this parenting journey alone; she needs you on her team.
- Keep talks light, simple, and free of criticism.
- Be her friend before being her adviser.

The (un)Natural Mom from Palm-Rose Plaza

Megan and Jessica rolled into one would be a ball of fire and action. Palm-Rose moms are activators, doers, and people movers. They have their families on a fast track to bigger and better things, with Megan's impatience and Jessica's positivity. Palm-Rose moms are not good at occupying backseats during meetings or working behind the scenes on anything like the Mothers of Chess Players League. They want to be where the excitement and the opportunities are.

Palm-Rose moms will run their children like a Little League team, cheering them all the way. They'll find this joyful purpose fulfilling in itself, unless their household is not keen on their goals. If that's the case, they may need a bit of a diversion in the form of a job with more enthusiastic colleagues.

Palm-Rose moms can have expectations as high as the pure Rose Bush moms, but thanks to the Palm influence, they aren't sullen or serious about these standards; they are motivating and inspiring. As long as their kids are happy and performing and making the most of every opportunity, they will likely be happy mothers.

They are often resented by moms who feel as if their lives have come to a halt. Palm-Rose moms seem to ignore the stop signs and red lights of life. Their high energy levels are especially intimidating. Their conspicuous successes make them seem lucky. Their optimism makes it easy for the rest of us to forget that they also go home to dirty laundry, pet-stained carpets, and children with inexplicable rashes. They also feel trapped at times, but they're masters of the game face. They're not false—just very brave.

The Palm-Rose mom also

- Finds silver linings even in failed math tests, relocations to a new country, and broken bones.
- Almost enjoys an argument or conflict without seeing that it can be hurtful.
- Does not accept no for an answer and will try to manipulate others into a yes. (It's okay to say no to her when she does this!)
- Can keep up with people half her age.
- Likes outdoor activities and challenges and is less hyper, driven, and negative after intense exercise.
- Complains that she has too much to do while clearly thriving on all the action and pressure.
- Tests authority and avoids strict authority figures, which could mean that submitting to her husband's decisions is especially hard for her.
- Has difficulty with waiting (for a toddler to go potty, for instance) and needs God's help with keeping her self-control.
- Tends to "have a better plan" before having heard what you suggested.
- Impulsively starts new initiatives and gets others on board, then suddenly loses interest and leaves others holding the bag.

To express love to a Palm-Rose,

- Tell her friends and her children good things about her. She needs to know that she has a powerful positive influence on people.
- Let her participate in intellectual and physical competitions. She thrives on the adrenaline more than on being number one.
- Point out when she acts like a bully or teases others about shortcomings. She'll like you even more if you can hold your ground against her.
- Let her take on multiple projects at once. Trying to calm her down and forcing her to rest or avoid risk is like putting a speedboat to anchor.
- Let her lead a large group of people without accusing her of being bossy. She's trying to help everyone succeed together.
- Take over some of her routine tasks. Any support that enables her to get the job done faster is an act of love.
- Give her prizes and rewards. (Even God promises rewards for us in heaven, doesn't He?)
- Let her do practical, active work even though she's a mommy. If you have traditional ideas about what a woman should or should not do, this may be a stretch for you. Reread the story of Deborah and Jael in the book of Judges!
- Let her have adventures, even without you. Pray for her when she goes out on these. Her fearless and passionate nature is open to temptation.

To help her be natural,

- Allow her to show how she feels, and remember that her expressions are "louder" than she intends them to be.
- If she fights you when you offer input, use the successes of her role models to influence the way she thinks.
- Don't get angry when she wants to debate things. It's how she comes up with her best ideas. You can agree to disagree with her.
- Let her lead and take a stand on the stage. Being in the spotlight is not about her ego; it's about her impact.
- Don't expect her to be silent and calm. Interpret her intensity as passion, not pressure.
- Let her apply new ideas and methods, as she thrives on innovation.
- Give her positive encouragement to do better; she loves a challenge.
- Give her a say in decisions or she may become negative.

The (un)Natural Mom on Box-Pine Pike

Boxwoods and Pine Trees enjoy gathering in the quieter and serene corner of the woods, unlike the Roses and Palms, who need as much action as possible. Leanne with her meticulous perfection and Penny with her peace and grace rolled into one will be a mom who loves to do things right but is in no hurry to get to that place of perfection. She will take herself and her children toward growth and learning in baby steps. She will strive to find easier, healthier, simpler ways to do everything from housework to menu planning. She will have a knack for systems that work.

She is likely to make a low-key impression on other moms. They will think she isn't playing the game all out, simply because she will be the last one to strive for first place or jump up in a parent-teacher meeting. She will sit, listen, process, and probably blush for the sake of the shameless moms who lose their cool next to the sports field. Being the disciplined and self-controlled mothering type that she is, she will seem to have an enviable maturity.

Remember Candice, who physically intervened in the argument over the ballet shoes? The Box-Pine mom would rather die than act like her and is likely to avoid moms like Candice in their inner circle. Box-Pine moms often feel unsafe around and even inferior to the fire-breathing-dragon moms.

Box-Pine moms are easily shamed and insulted. They know when people spread gossip about them. They notice the looks and whispers. They seem to be untouched and even snobbish because they don't stoop to having fights or confrontations about these rumors, but they are in reality hurt by their inability to be the social butterfly who throws caution to the wind. Caution is their middle name!

They have a fishnet-like awareness that lets nothing get past them. If anyone is at odds with anybody else, they know about it, mourn it, and feel obligated to try to reconcile the two parties. It should come as no surprise that Box-Pine moms use calm reason and patient negotiation to convince their children to obey, play nicely together, and do what will not "break her heart."

The Box-Pine mom also
- Prefers indoor activities, such as crafts, blogging, reading, and puzzles.

- Keeps records of details so that she can use her notes as a step-by-step plan.
- Sets an example to other wives in how she cooperates with her husband.
- Avoids the limelight and shields her children from public failure that could harm their self-esteem.
- Can be finicky about manners due to her love of order and her fear of criticism.
- Avoids large or loud groups in which the tempers and decibels tend to flare up (such as next to the football field).
- Is introverted and may even be shy. (These two things are not the same!)
- Takes meticulous care of her treasured possessions. (Luckily for her spouse and kids, she views them in this category.)
- Dislikes sudden changes and needs time to adapt.
- Keeps correcting and improving her work, which leads to difficulty finishing.
- Seems unapproachable and withdrawn but is often just deep in thought.

To show love to a Box-Pine,
- Allow her to choose who she wants to be with and when. Her social capacity is small when it comes to strangers. Only close friends recharge her.
- Let her be a spectator rather than a participant in sports or games with fierce competition and potentially painful physical contact.

- Give her time to think about choices, changes, and risks that need to be weighed. Don't mock her meticulous analysis and preparation, even if you think she over-prepares. It's how she builds confidence to take risks.
- Be patient while she struggles to talk about her emotions. Don't judge or interrupt, and gently reflect what you hear until she says, "You understand."
- Make some of the big decisions that need to be settled in a hurry. She'd forgive you more easily for a mistake than she'd forgive herself for a wrong decision.
- Support her effort to clean up and declutter her life and environment. Refrain from giving your opinion about her many files, boxes, and labels. Accept that she needs them, or she might file you away in a folder marked "Undesirables."
- Give her a system or plan to work by, such as a Bible study, an online guide, or a schedule (unless it is a diet plan, of course).
- Give only the most essential correction and in a soft voice. She takes all negative words seriously, and a little pain goes a long way.
- Put in writing what you appreciate about her. (The Mother's Day cards are not wasted on her! A hand-made card with a lot of words will earn you a thousand points.)
- Facilitate some quiet time for her in a peaceful environment. (Start by holding the baby so she can go to the bathroom alone!)

To help her be natural,

- Get your timing right when you need her to do something outside her comfort zone. Granted, it can be like waiting for a ripening avocado: not yet ... almost ... oops, too late!
- Help make things around her fairly stable and consistent (what you would call *boring*).
- Let her learn by watching others; she's not one to be pushed into the deep end. You'll have a drowning on your hands.
- Suggest a role model who is sensitive and fair or a mentor she can use as a sounding board.
- Don't change things without good reason and advance notice. She'll feel disrespected.
- Make it clear what is expected of her and thank her when she meets those expectations. She hates guesswork.
- Allow her to exclude from your weekend or holiday plans people who drain her.
- Allow her to clarify the rules and limits before she agrees to take on an important task (such as knowing the exact scope of work when she helps a child study for a test).
- Ask what you can do to help her, but don't barge in. Her systems and plans are delicate.
- Help her divide tasks into steps when she gets overwhelmed. If she starts worrying about varsity fees while her children are still babies, help her set a goal for five years rather than for fifteen or twenty.

The (un)Natural Mom from Pine-Rose Place

Pine-Roses are a combination of the two rational thinkers. Can you imagine Megan and Penny in a blend? One would be forgiven for wondering if it is even possible! It is, and these moms have a beautiful intermingling of Megan's drive and Penny's compassion. They speak with restraint, but when they speak, they command respect. Pine-Rose moms are not the frilly-dress moms, to understate matters. They avoid "estrogen fests," such as ladies' retreats and mosaic workshops. They are likely to prefer male company to the chatter of hatted ladies at a women's tea.

The idea of being nominated to assist backstage with ballerina hairdos or fairy costumes probably is scarier to her than a visit to the dentist. But give this mom the stage manager's position. Her natural gift of taking charge in a calm and controlled manner will make the whole process flow according to plan without her seeming bossy or nosy. She is not the mom who will remind your little angel to smile and wave to the audience, though, because this is exactly what she cares about the least: amateur entertainment, appearances, and impressing people.

Pine-Rose moms can be stubborn and independent. Getting them truly involved in pure fun will be a challenge. Getting a lively chitchat going with them about children's clothing or lunch-box ideas is an impossibly high aspiration. They will have one or two topics that they love to talk about, though, and a true friend will find those in time.

Practical and pragmatic, she will play in her children's lives only those parts that she feels she can play well. She'll be able to delegate with ease, however, firmly believing that one should not meddle where others can do better. This may lead her to employ helpers in areas where her children could have benefited from more closeness to her.

Pine-Roses are often said to have a CEO temperament. They are the calm leaders who keep goals and the welfare of their teams in balance. In a Pine-Rose mom's life, this means that she has high hopes for her family but will not drive her children to achievement for the sake of achievement if she sees them suffering for it.

The fact that she is the least emotional of all the parenting types means that she could seem and function more like a typical dad than a mom. She might be a little aloof and hands-off. We often see her choosing a more emotional husband, who takes on the emotional and nurturing roles within the household while she often pursues a career in a field traditionally occupied by men.

Even if she chooses to be a stay-at-home mom, the Pine-Rose mom tends to look like either an executive or a no-nonsense tomboy. Don't underestimate her mothering strengths based on either.

The Pine-Rose mom also
- Finds it hard to cooperate when she's angry or disappointed; she tends to clam up.
- Has a difficult time taking the first step in building or restoring a relationship. *Sorry* is the hardest word for her to say!
- Is independent to the point that she operates as a single parent even when she's married.
- Becomes annoyed with a barrage of why, how, and when questions.

- Keeps her emotions about herself and her kids hidden as well as she can.
- Stays focused on what really matters without sweating the small stuff.
- Seems blunt or standoffish at times if you don't know her well.
- Is stripped-down and grounded; she doesn't fuss.
- Parents from her gut without speaking much.
- Can handle tons of pressure without cracking.
- Doesn't enjoy displays of wild emotion.
- Responds thoughtfully but with candor.
- Is not trying to be the popular mom.
- Will do anything to protect her family.

To express love to a Pine-Rose,

- Remain consistent and calm toward her. She experiences "mental seasickness" when you make too many waves. Explain your feelings to her rather than letting them explode.
- Give her a break from attending to details and the nitty-gritty daily needs in the household.
- Refrain from threatening and pressuring her. Nothing changes her attitude from willing to unwilling faster than a forceful approach.
- Privately acknowledge her achievements, without fanfare, fuss, or tears.
- Say clearly what you expect of her. She believes this saying: "There is no expectation without words."

- Allow her to back out of unnecessary social events. She can network with people toward a purpose, but she can't do what she calls "pointless mingling at the punch bowl."
- Let her ask the purpose and meaning of things. She can work relentlessly toward a worthwhile goal, but only if it makes sense to her.
- Let her be alone after stressful times. She doesn't need a sounding board; she needs solitude.
- Don't interrupt her work. To her, it is the ultimate disrespect.
- Help to keep the family atmosphere free of drama. She tends to forget that emotions bind people together. In her view, emotions accompany conflict and are unproductive.
- Allow her to lead in areas where she is naturally stronger. There's no need to be threatened by her. She easily steps back to let you dance when your song is playing.

To help her be natural,
- Remind her of the long-term reward of all the little motherhood chores.
- Give her the opportunity to make better plans when she has messed up.
- When talking to her about parenting, keep it short (but not sweet) and factual.
- Don't expect her to multitask. She'll focus and do the most important things first.

- Don't expect her to talk about things she's still figuring out. Wait for her to be ready.
- Understand that she is comfortable in a moms' group only when she can play a directing role.
- Spare her all the new fads, facts, and fancy things; she's not interested.
- Trust her love for you. She's loyal. Don't press her for proof.
- Avoid digging into the past. She'd rather forget and move on.

The (un)Natural Mom on Box-Palm Parade

Here's to the mom who has always wondered if she is two persons in one body, has a split personality, is bipolar, or should have herself admitted, when in fact she has the same tree type as David, a man after God's own heart! Like him, the precious Box-Palm mom can be down in the dumps one minute, singing the blues (some of David's blue psalms will do just fine), and dancing the next with such exuberance that certain items of clothing may become optional. David and the Box-Palm mom have both been given disapproving looks by the likes of David's wife Michal, who could not respect his dramatic flair. Instead of telling David to become more dignified, God locked Michal's womb (2 Sam. 6).

Box-Palm mothers are the most passionate and colorful. They have innumerable shades of joy and sadness and the capacity to feel both deep despair and euphoric joy in short succession.

Box-Palm mothers often remember the details of every significant mothering event and keep mementos. When asked to be less intense, they feel dismissed. In their desire to please and act appropriately, they never know which side of themselves to show to an often judgmental world.

When it comes to disciplining kids, they are often torn between their Boxwood love for order and their Palm Tree love of joy. They may jump from program to program in search of the latest fix, not sure they can trust their own ever-changing ideas.

The Box-Palm mom holds between her tears and her laughter many precious gifts: artistry, creativity, poetry, appreciation for all things human and heavenly, and passion like a fountain.

A Box-Palm mom also

- Tends to be dramatic and irrational during arguments or under pressure.
- Interprets a child's disobedience or negativity as rejection or even hatred.
- Is curious and interested in all things new and exciting, to the point where she can get caught up in extremes and even spiritually risky ideas or activities.
- Can be temperamental and unpredictable, needing solitude one minute and an audience the next.
- May use emotional manipulation as a weapon on her kids.
- Chats excitedly about new ideas, creations, people, and plans in colorful language.
- May seem as if she is wearing a mask but is in fact unable to hide what she feels: a brutal vulnerability.
- Is torn between wanting to be more "normal" and wanting to stand out as a unique individual.

- Craves order but is unable to sustain it.
- Is inspiring and impressive—not a person you forget once you've had the privilege of meeting her.
- Might exaggerate when she tells a story, because how it felt weighs more than how it happened.
- Gets excited easily, which can make discipline more heated than it needs to be or so funny that she can't get her point across.
- Tends to base her faith on her heart rather than her head—that is, on feelings rather than facts.

To express love to a Box-Palm,
- Accept her fluctuating emotions and diverse interests. She needs you to stretch your embrace around all of it.
- Allow and facilitate opportunities for her creative self-expression.
- Spoil her with elaborate, sentimental surprises. She will savor every detail and remember them forever!
- Give her enthusiastic, strongly worded encouragement and compliments. "Nice job, honey" is not specific enough.
- Refrain from correcting her publicly.
- Let her talk freely about her ideas without pointing out irrational, impractical, unlikely, unaffordable, and inaccurate elements. She will come up with something amazing when she can start in the land of endless possibility.

- Let her have fun in any silly way she needs to. It's not easy to be a carefree child and a deeply concerned woman rolled into one. She needs play to balance herself.

To help her be natural,
- Allow her to adapt her workplace and home to suit her mood.
- Let her talk and move and write and create all at once if that works for her.
- Don't box her in with a strict routine. If you like routine, be the one to implement it for yourself and the children.
- Don't criticize her for being scatterbrained. The more she feels unloved, the worse her concentration and memory will be.
- Encourage her originality and inventiveness.
- Believe her feelings even when her words don't make much sense.
- Ensure that she has a creative outlet.
- Allow her to feel emotional extremes.
- Pray for her to escape from her depressed times and to rediscover joy.

For Reflection

1. How has this book affected your view of mothers whose parenting styles are different from yours?

2. Think of a mom you avoid or have difficulty understanding. Which temperament do you think she might be? Name two aspects of her temperament that could be considered strengths. How might you pray for her?

3. Name something you have learned about yourself that you didn't know before taking the Tall Trees Parenting Profile and reading this book.

4. If you could pick one of these combination tree types to be your mother, which one would be best suited to you? Why do you think so?

5. Write down three aspects of your own temperament that you can celebrate and affirm when you worry about whether you're mothering well.

9

The Call to (super)Natural Motherhood

Many years ago as a newlywed at age twenty-one, I sat on the couch of a psychiatrist, smoking—not smoking a cigarette but smoking from burnout. He listened patiently as I read my homework. The previous week, he had sent me home with a curious assignment: "Start at your earliest memory and write all the significant episodes of your life until this day." The task had taken me a whole day. I cried myself dry as I remembered things I had buried under layers of decency and denial. As I read those pages aloud, he nodded; then he took them from me and used a highlighter to mark several words on each page. He handed my autobiography back to me with sincere tears in his eyes. He had highlighted only one word and one phrase that occurred dozens of times throughout my scribblings: *must* and *had to*.

I looked at my story with new insight. So many demands. So much pressure. So much striving. Then he asked his first question: "Who is calling you to all these things, telling you what you have to do and who you need to be?"

I started weeping. "Everyone! My parents, my husband, my university lecturers … I have to be perfect, be a friend, a daughter, a wife, a top student. It's just so hard to be all these things! There are days when I think I hear my name and I swing around, thinking I've dropped something or done something wrong, only to see that no one is behind me."

I think he fired an arrow prayer to heaven and got an instant answer. He asked, "Who first called you by your name?"

With just two questions, I saw the match that the Enemy loves to set to the dry wood of our lives. He plagues us with the message that we don't and won't make it. This lie doesn't suddenly start when we are mothers, but motherhood often adds just enough friction to ignite the match.

Similar questions are important for all mothers:

1. Who gets to say what the perfect mother should be and do?
2. Who first called us by the name Mom?

Typically, our idea of the perfect mother is a collection of requirements handed down by people around us. Some of these ideas may be close to God's, but many are mere cultural tapestries thick with dust and myths. Unraveling these to test each idea against God's Word is worthwhile. This is tricky, of course. It is a journey each mother should embark upon with wise women to guide her as she prays and asks God for answers to this first question.

In regard to the second question, we are mistaken if we think that our first calling comes from society or our children. It was not when others congratulated you on your baby's birth that you were first called a mother; it wasn't when your own child said *Mama* for the first time either. Our first calling came from God Himself. When

He allowed you to conceive a child, whether in your own body or not, He called you Mom, long before anybody knew.

Only the One who calls us by name has the right to tell us how we should be. The beauty is that He does not tell us without enabling us as well. He doesn't demand what we don't have. And we always have enough by virtue of His free gifts.

The Bible tells many birth stories in which God is an active participant who speaks and guides. He gives names and special callings for the children, and special duties and instructions to the parents. He even tells the mothers secrets about the future that He wants them to keep in mind as they raise their children. Read the stories of Hagar (Gen. 16; 21), Rebekah (Gen. 25:21–23), Hannah (1 Sam. 1–2), Elizabeth (Luke 1), and Mary (Luke 1:26–38) for examples of this. We don't have a record of God's words to Hannah, but her inspiration to dedicate her son to God's temple clearly came from Him. Elizabeth probably received her parenting instructions from her husband, Zechariah, who in turn received many details about their son's future and upbringing from an angel (Luke 1:13–20).

God called these (un)Natural Moms to (super)Natural Motherhood. This is a call to trust that God has not made a mistake in choosing you to be the mother to your children. When we answer this call, we agree that God has a magnificent destiny for our families. When we answer the call, we say yes to a journey that may be tough at times.

I am willing to bet that Hagar felt like an (un)Natural Mom every day. Forced to become Abraham's wife, chased away twice, and hated by her master's wife, her rejection as a woman and mother was severe. And still, God assured her more than once that she was His

Plan A mom for Ishmael and that He had an inheritance for her and her son.

Rebekah would have felt like an utter failure as a mother of sons who gave new meaning to the term *sibling rivalry* if God had not told her that He made them enemies when they were still in her womb. Her son Jacob would have brought her great shame through all of his cheating and conniving, but even when God named him, it was already clear that his life had been scripted. Had Rebekah been as strict about justice as our dear Leanne, she never would have let the blessing of the firstborn Esau go to Jacob. She would have interfered with God's plan by "setting right" what God had decided to turn upside down for a reason only He could see. Fortunately, by design, Rebekah showed one of the traits we despise in a mother: she had a favorite! God used even that to bring His eternal plans to fruition.

Hannah's prayer to have a child, coupled with the promise to give him away again, seems completely unnatural too. Who begs to have a son to give up? Although Samuel was the desire of her heart, she was able to take him to Eli when he was just weaned and to sing an exuberant song of praise as she left him there. What unnatural strength! When we look at Samuel's journey, we know why God chose a mother such as Hannah, who could do what many mothers have to do: give a child away. God led her to do this because Samuel was destined to be a great prophet. Hannah could not have led Samuel into his destiny on her own. He needed training in the temple with Eli as his mentor as he grew in his prophetic gift. Although Hannah had her reasons (gratitude and the keeping of a promise), God was really behind it all. I often wish that those who are quick to judge a mother who gives up a child would see this story of Hannah as a model for adoption.

Hannah, Elizabeth (the mother of John the Baptist), and Mary (the mother of Jesus) all sing to God or recite words of praise as they have an expectation of the great plans God has *for* their children or for the good of the world *through* their children. They worship in spite of shame, pain, and ridicule because they understand the call to (super) Natural Motherhood. They understand that they, as ordinary as they are, are part of a master plan. They know that their children's journeys do not depend as much on them doing everything right as they do on God giving them the assurance that He will never make a mistake.

Rebirth into (super)Natural Motherhood

Natural Motherhood is tough. It demands we be put together and in control at all times. To be the Natural Mother culture expects us to be, we can't be honest about our recurrent desire to run away from home or to hide the mistakes we have made with our children. Every day is an act. We put on our motherhood makeup, painting on a confidence that is only external and a smile that needs lip gloss to be convincing. If this is what's required to be "natural," who could possibly be a (super)Natural Mother?

Far from keeping it all together at all times, I believe the starting point of (super)Natural Motherhood is the exact opposite. I believe that if a Natural Mother can be born, a (super)Natural Mom must be reborn. This rebirth comes when something in a mother dies. What needs to die is all the striving to "keep it all together," which looks different for each type of mother. Paul says it so beautifully when he calls us breakable vessels of clay carrying inside of us a treasure of great worth (2 Cor. 4:7). A treasure can leak out only when the clay pot cracks.

This is my conviction: every (un)Natural Mom needs to crack in order to become a (super)Natural Mom. Some of us have cracked more than once, and what came out of us did not look or sound like a treasure. These crash-and-burn episodes are often the result of our not having the support we need or not leaning on God when we should. I believe that God is after a different kind of "cracking." He is interested in the cracks that we don't try to hide—the honesty with which we acknowledge that we are often not okay. Out of this kind of crack flows a myriad of treasures: humility, honesty, true remorse, new hope.

But even this cracking is not rebirth. It's only the first sign. The clues to the kind of cracking that brings true breakthrough are in the songs of Hannah, Elizabeth, and Mary. Here are a few snippets to consider:

> Nothing and no one is holy like GOD,
>> no rock mountain like our God.
> Don't dare talk pretentiously—
>> not a word of boasting, ever!
> For GOD knows what's going on....
> He puts poor people on their feet again;
>> he rekindles burned-out lives with fresh hope,
> Restoring dignity and respect to their lives—
>> a place in the sun! (Hannah, 1 Sam. 2:2–3, 8)

> Yes, I see it all now:
>> I'm the Lord's maid, ready to serve.

Let it be with me
    just as you say. (Mary, Luke 1:38)

Blessed woman, who believed what God said,
    believed every word would come true!
        (Elizabeth, Luke 1:45)

I'm bursting with God-news;
    I'm dancing the song of my Savior God....
He bared his arm and showed his strength,
    scattered the bluffing braggarts.
He knocked tyrants off their high horses,
    pulled victims out of the mud.
The starving poor sat down to a banquet;
    the callous rich were left out in the cold.
He remembered his chosen child, Israel;
    he remembered and piled on the mercies, piled
        them high.
It's exactly what he promised,
    beginning with Abraham and right up to now.
        (Mary, Luke 1:46, 51–55)

These heart songs don't sound like Jessica's chirpy limerick, yet they ooze joy. There is no mention of a pregnancy or baby. There is no trace of concern for what people will think of them or their children or what would become of their dreams. No mention of private schooling, violin lessons, tennis coaching, or a trust fund. The songs are God songs.

I read a number of truths in them:

1. A (super)Natural Mom knows that God writes the story.
When we don't know what's going on and we feel like a mismatch with our kids, God is the One who knows the end from the beginning. He knows whether we are to shape one another or to cheer one another on. He knows whether we will be instrumental in bringing one another to breaking points—the good kind—or to victory. It's not our task to figure it out. It's merely our task to trust the Author of our life story.

2. A (super)Natural Mom realizes that the foremost agenda is God's salvation demonstrated throughout the earth.
Family breakdowns are often the backdrop to God's salvation stories. Think of the story of Joseph, for instance. A father showed such favoritism to his son that he became his siblings' target. The son had such a sense of entitlement that he became an unbearable brat. His brothers had so little compassion that they sold him as a slave and had so little respect for their father that they fabricated false proof of his son's death that broke the man's heart (Gen. 37). Every one of us should instantly feel a lot better about our households.

This parenting disaster sets the stage for Joseph to end up in Egypt, where his gifts of dreams and strategy save millions of lives (Gen. 39–41).

Jacob, who became Israel—the father of the twelve tribes of God's chosen nation—has a background riddled with brokenness and shame. Moses, used by God to save millions, was an adopted boy whose father never figured into his life. Jesus was also adopted and most likely lost His father before going into ministry. None of these boys had a simple life in an ideal nuclear family, but God used them to be saviors.

A (super)Natural Mom keeps this perspective and always knows that any child of any mom can be part of God's salvation story. God has all of us on display to a world desperately in need of seeing Him in us—not just His heart but also His hand. "He bared his arm and showed his strength," Mary sang. Do you realize that when we go all pear shaped in our homes and we and our children are in trouble, God has an ideal canvas to paint salvation stories on?

3. A (super)Natural Mom is delighted to play a part in God's story no matter how hard.

Imagine you were the mother of the blind man Jesus healed (Mark 8:22–25). Your life was tough from the moment he was born. You could never leave him alone for a minute for fear that he could hurt himself or break something. When your friends' sons started helping them in the field and bringing food and earnings into their households, you made the painful decision to put your son at the city gate to beg. This was never your dream. You asked many questions about the reason for this unfair disadvantage. You cried when you thought of his future. You blushed as the legalists made the conclusion that his blindness was definitely the result of your sin. And then one day you heard the truth: "Jesus said, 'You're asking the wrong question. You're looking for someone to blame. There is no such cause-effect here. Look instead for what God can do'" (John 9:3).

Your tough journey through motherhood with a child who made it hard had nothing to do with what either of you deserved. It was all for the sake of a miracle that had never been seen before: the healing of a man born blind. It was all to point others to a God they needed to know as the One who could do anything.

Can you make peace with such a life story? Can you suffer for the sake of God's glory?

Are we able to echo Mary's commitment to submit to whatever God wants to do, however He wants to use us, even if that means a tough journey through motherhood? This is what a (super)Natural Mom does: she steps onto God's stage and puts out her hand in faith for a script she has not read, willing to play whatever part He assigns to her.

4. A (super)Natural Mom knows that building her own bright future while disregarding God will lead nowhere.
We all have plans and ideas about what the best future for our family should look like. Some of us "work [our] worried fingers to the bone" (Ps. 127:2), trying to build this future. We are in danger of becoming self-made supermoms who need to heed Hannah's warning, "Don't

dare talk pretentiously—not a word of boasting, ever!" We could become the "bluffing braggarts" of Mary's song too. Sometimes the images that mothers build up about their families on social media resemble these terms, don't they? Medals, models, and med-school graduates are paraded without a hint of humility. But there are some moms who caption these pictures with words of gratitude that acknowledge that all the achievements are by grace. They are (super)Natural Moms.

5. A (super)Natural Mom knows she can't fill burned-out lives with new hope but trusts that God can.
If we believe that it is our job to right everything that has gone wrong with our children, we will burn out, guaranteed. We can try our best to restore joy to a child with depression or to instill courage in a child who has given up, but in the end only God can restore a child's soul. This is where we have an opportunity to put our children in God's lap so that He can fill us and our children with new hope.

6. A (super)Natural Mom knows that she doesn't give her children a place in the sun; God does.
I love these words of Hannah: "Restoring dignity and respect to their lives—a place in the sun!" Supermoms fight for this and often exhibit their worst behavior in the process, thinking it their duty to drag others into the shadows so there will be standing room for their children

in the sun. Or they collect the material things and status symbols that should grant their children respect and dignity.

A (super)Natural Mom has a different perspective. She knows that the sun in question is the favor of God and that her children can bask in it anywhere they stand, whether privileged or poor. Instead of buying designer outfits, she dresses her children in a unique type of dignity: a metaphorical brand called "highly favored."

7. A (super)Natural Mom knows that her failures won't stop God from keeping all the promises He made concerning her life and the lives of her children.

"Blessed woman who believed what God said, believed every word would come true!" Elizabeth's heart sings, and Mary makes a declaration of faith to echo this: "He remembered his chosen child, Israel; He remembered and piled on the mercies, piled them high. It's exactly what he promised, beginning with Abraham and right up to now." Israel and their many failures, their flawed kings and even more corrupt princes, could not destroy what God had covenanted with Abraham: blessing to all His spiritual children!

A (super)Natural Mom knows that her children who have put their faith in Christ are heirs to the same blessing. She is more concerned that her children find this righteousness than she is about doing everything right. She listens for individual promises God makes to her and her children, knowing that He still speaks and desires to tell us secrets, saying to us as He did to Jeremiah, "Call to me and I will answer you. I'll tell you marvelous and wondrous things that you could never figure out on your own" (Jer. 33:3).

Giving Up the (un)Natural and the Natural

Each of these biblical women was partly a natural match and partly an unnatural match for the path God chose for her. Mary would have been right at home at Pine Tree Place. Not known for many words but rather for keeping words deep in her heart and pondering them, she was caring and submissive. If there is a mother who should not see her child suffer as Mary had to see Jesus do on the cross, it is a Pine Tree mom. Here was the ultimate nurturer, watching her son being torn to pieces. One would think it would break her, but it didn't. A Rose Bush mom probably would have fought tooth and nail, yelling, "Over my dead body," and would have gotten her wish. A Boxwood mom would have struggled with the injustice to the point that she may never have forgiven God. A Palm Tree mom's performance would have rivaled only Peter's Palm Tree drama at Gethsemane. Although Mary's heart was shattered, she had the design to accept the pain, knowing that it was prophesied from the beginning (Luke 2:34–35). She could fall into the arms of John, the new son Jesus gave her as comfort (John 19:26–27).

Mary cracked long before she saw her son die. She cracked when she surrendered herself to God's plan the day the angel Gabriel brought the message that she would bear the Savior. It was unplanned, it was uncomfortable, it was inexplicable, but she accepted it. I have seen many Pine Tree moms walk this same journey: raising children who put them through excruciating pain they did not deserve or cause. When they crack in the way Mary did—by proclaiming themselves to be vessels of God's higher plans—they find joy on the other side of their hardship and sometimes even in the midst of it.

Palm Tree moms and Rose Bush moms don't crack in the same way as the Pine Trees, and Boxwood moms have their own journey too. The things that bring them each to their cracking points also differ dramatically. Each has to give up on her need to have the perfect story the way she would like it.

Here I may seem to contradict every previous chapter. I went to great lengths to defend every kind of (un)Natural Mom. I gave their families tips to help the mothers be more natural, urged their children and spouses to validate and attempt to fulfill their unique needs, only to say now that in order to be (super)Natural, every mom needs to let all her ideals go. Yes. Why? Because it is virtually impossible to become selfless before clearly seeing the self that we have been preserving and defending all along.

Only when we see ourselves clearly, embrace our value and our fallibility alike, are we ready to embrace growth. That is why I scripted confessions as well as affirmations in the previous chapters. Only treasured and forgiven women can find the courage to venture where they may be denied what they love the most. Once they do, miracles happen. The Boxwood Trees still live on Boxwood Boulevard and keep their Boxwood nature, but they break free from the need to control all the details; Rose Bushes keep their strength, but a new level of trust in God rather than in themselves sets in; Palm

Trees become anchored in principle and faithfulness without losing their childlike joy; and the Pines step out of their comfort zone to walk on water.

Testimony of a (super)Natural Palm Tree Mom

I grew up with an alcoholic mom. She became extremely abusive and neglectful whenever she had too much to drink. I was the middle child but, being a creative Palm Tree who could think fast on my feet, I made up games and stories to protect my siblings. I would tell them, for example, that our mom had sent us to the store to buy a can of baked beans. I'd gather a few coins and take them with me to the store. We'd walk and sing and I would entertain them and make sure that we stayed away as long as possible. I knew that after the drunken frenzy, our mom would pass out and be harmless for the night. When we got home, I'd share the baked beans among us as if it were a feast for kings. This role of joy bringer suited me and became my identity.

Then I became a mom and vowed, of course, that I would never be like my mom. And I wasn't. I was the complete opposite. I would do anything for my kids. I was always present and always nurturing. Then one day the worst thing that could ever happen happened: our oldest daughter died in an accident. Even now the story is hard for me to tell in detail. I had failed as the joy bringer! I went into deep depression.

Patiently, God lifted me out of the sea of despair and restored me as a mom. I resumed my aim to keep my two surviving daughters happy at all times, never realizing that this had remained my highest goal as a mother and that it was the very thing that needed to be broken in me. The oldest of the two developed a strong will, with which she held me hostage. I felt absolutely ineffective as a mom. I wanted to be a good mom who trained her children to behave well, but I just couldn't discipline her.

At my low point, God showed me the belief that had taken over my life: *I have to make everybody happy at all times.* It sounded like the truth but was in fact a lie that resonated with my Palm Tree nature. I had to give up my main aim—never to cause tears—in order to become a good mom. The first time I was able to punish one of my daughters for blatantly disobeying me, I experienced a new kind of joy. I then became a mom who did what God expected even when it meant going against what came naturally. My daughter changed. She had wanted a firmer hand all along. Her out-of-control behavior improved dramatically as she started trusting me to be consistent and firm and set boundaries for her. She is a serious child. My Palm Tree nature sometimes clashes with hers, but because I always see the glass half full, I can be an encourager to her. I am the perfect mom for my daughters.

Testimony of a (super)Natural Pine Tree Mom

I need harmony and security in my home. I did not grow up with this stability at all, which made me want it even more for my family. My greatest wish for my children was that we would provide them with a secure future. We lived our dream for many years. My husband became a successful businessman and we had more than we needed. I could give my children many privileges I never enjoyed.

In the span of two years, everything collapsed. It started with nonpayment of a large government project my husband had worked on for years. Instead of being set for life, we were soon scraping together money for our daily needs and figuring out how to keep our house and cars.

To add to the disruption, we received devastating news about our children's health: first my oldest, then my youngest. They would need expensive medication for a chronic condition for the rest of their lives.

Now, years later, we are still taking one day at a time. I have to get up every night to administer medication. I can't remember the last time I slept through the night. Pine Trees need their rest, but I have little. I had to reach out for help from others.

When I meet with mothers of children who have the same medical condition, they often ask why I'm not crying and rebelling. On the night my youngest was diagnosed, I surrendered her to God the way Abraham surrendered Isaac. She was in a coma and I lay in the hospital bed next to her, weeping before God. I knew I had to give her to God too, just as I had done with my oldest. He would be their safe place. There was nothing I could do to guarantee a long life for them. He gave me a guarantee of their security in His arms for eternity. What I dreamed for them, they could still have! That is the peace I return to when the illness breathes fear into my heart.

I am designed for a long journey of faith, like the journey of Abraham, my fellow Pine Tree. This is such a long journey. I have the patience and contentment that is needed. My nurturing mothering style has been a saving grace too. Taking care of those around me, keeping an eye on their needs, comes naturally for me. This is probably why my friends constantly say that they are glad my daughters have me for a mother.

Testimony of a (super)Natural Rose Bush Mom

God called me to lead children to Christ when I was thirteen. It was all I ever wanted to do with my life. I wrote programs for churches at a young age and taught people much older than I how to work effectively with youth. I married a gentle man who shared my love for children.

We decided to adopt after years of trying in vain to get pregnant. We adopted a boy with a disability and, two years later, one of mixed race. My fearless can-do attitude toward life probably contributed to my determination to adopt the children who may not be chosen first. Quite unexpectedly, I became pregnant with our third son a few years later.

Our three boys grew up in the slipstream of my philosophy. I never let them believe they were anything but valuable, equally loved, chosen, and able to do whatever they set their minds to. I encouraged them to participate in sports and cultural activities, and they all excelled in spite of prejudicial perceptions and often discrimination too. We used everything we had learned about working with young people to give our kids the best possible life. We raised them with God in the center of our household.

Many parents thought we were living a fairy tale and responded to me as if I were Mother Teresa. Little did they know that things had become complicated. Our oldest son was giving us a hard time. His disability had become a social challenge as well as an academic one. I became the target of his adolescent mood swings, and he blamed me for every bit of unhappiness in his life, of which his being adopted had become the epicenter. His anger became so intense that I once ended up in the ER for stitches.

Thanks to the Rose Bush in me, I have always been able to put my hurt and disappointment in one box and my love for my troubled son in another. I refused to give up on him even when everyone advised me to take drastic steps. My Rose Bush determination to make things work led us to every reputable therapist's door, to every seminar on my son's disability, to every educational option for him, and back again to ground zero. The top psychiatrists did their best too. No matter what we did right and what help I enlisted, our son's behavior seemed to deteriorate rather than improve. What worked for other people simply did not work for us.

A turning point came when a behavioral expert explained to me that my son's conduct has always been his to choose. It has always been beyond my control. I cannot make him do what I want him to do. He is not the product of me and my mothering. When I look at my other children, the proof of my intentional and dedicated mothering is clearly there. It is not my fault.

I am now on a journey to let go. God is my strength, and I did reach the point where I enlisted all the help I could get, quite a victory for a Rose Bush mom. I will surrender so that God can do this, however hard it may be for me. That is why I am the chosen mom for these boys.

Testimony of a (super)Natural Boxwood Mom

I am a trained psychologist. I married late and had my daughter at age thirty-six. I planned to enjoy being pregnant, but the morning sickness hit and I was constantly throwing up. My husband supported me as best he could, but I cried every day, being unable to do all the tasks I needed to do and feeling so sick. I couldn't wait to be me again.

I wanted to go back to living my motto: "The only thing better than being up to date and on schedule is being *ahead* of schedule!"

After the first trimester, just as I felt I had my life back, my mom was diagnosed with oral cancer. We have no other family, so I had to be her support. She had to have a large section of her jaw and palate cut away, and I needed to be strong for her. My pregnancy plan, thought through in detail before I got pregnant, was to go shopping for baby clothes with my mom and rest at home. Instead, I was driving to the hospital three times a day, watching her suffer. I put on a strong, happy, positive face for her (which was extremely draining for a Boxwood like me) and then sobbed (which came naturally) as I walked out of the hospital.

More than anything, I was extremely concerned about the effect all of this stress would have on my baby. I had visited a psychologist friend once a month to get a grip on my stress and anxiety before I got pregnant so I could be calm during the pregnancy and after the birth. This had helped a great deal, but the curveball of my mother's poor health made me wonder if all these efforts to be stress-free would come undone. I understood my mother's trauma to be a real threat to my baby's health.

By grace my daughter turned out perfectly, though, and the planned C-section went well. My mom was soon cancer free, although traumatized and unable to eat much. I was, however, unable to rest as I should because I was unable to rest with any housework left undone. This led to unsuccessful breastfeeding, but a nurse gave me a charting method to improve my milk supply and make sure my daughter got enough. I got carried away making notes and lists. For eighteen months I recorded everything.

Things turned out well without any of my plans going exactly as I had hoped! I probably should have learned to leave space for life's unpredictability. Still, when I got pregnant for the second time, I reverted to my Boxwood Tree plans. I was determined to finish reading two informative baby books. I divided up the first book's chapters to read so I would be done before the baby arrived and planned to read the second book after the birth in order to keep up with my daughter's development.

Then I miscarried. The entire year I had planned out disappeared and was a blank.

My Boxwood notes and meticulous records about my first daughter's early months became a source of joy in the dark days. What may have seemed like obsessive scribbles to others became my daughter's life story and physical proof of my best efforts as a mother. Other moms might read fashion magazines, but I read those notes I had made. I marvel at how we survived those early weeks in spite of her waking up so many times each night; I revisit the details of how much she drank at each feeding. These tiny victories make me look forward to the future.

We don't know if God has another baby in His plans for us, but the journey so far has been worthwhile, regardless of the outcome. It has taught me that God's plans trump mine. I no longer question whether I had given up too easily on my lofty goals. Maybe good enough is fine, and perhaps I can stop trying for perfection.

Having survived the clash between the Boxwood ideal and real-life motherhood, I realize I am still a Boxwood mom who will make notes again, but no longer out of fear of failure or to prove myself. Now I will make notes as proof of God's goodness and keep records of His faithfulness as a monument of His love. One day my daughter will read these for herself. Rose Bush that she is, she'd probably need proof one day; Boxwood Tree that I am, I might even have a backup copy!

Giving Up the Supermom Struggle

Supermoms created by society receive the admiration a heroine deserves. It's all about the individual. But God gives us a different kind of superpower: He gives unique gifts as He sees fit, but never enough for us to be self-sufficient. He takes joy in building communities rather than Lone Rangers, interdependence rather than independence. In His models for marriage, family, and church, He never demands that an individual be the full package. In fact, He clearly warns us that we will never be everything or have it all apart from the "body" to which we belong and that without Him as our "head," we would wither (Rom. 12:5; Eph. 4:15–16 NIV).

(Super)Natural Motherhood, therefore, is never something you and I can live out all by ourselves. We will need people. We will need examples and mentors and helpers. A (super)Natural Mom will not try to do this alone. Every mom in the testimonies learned to lean on others as she grew from (un)Natural to (super)Natural. Mary stayed with Elizabeth for three months. I believe that is what it took for her to come to terms with her journey.

Giving Up the Improbable Ideal

(Super)Natural Motherhood accommodates needs, mistakes, divorce, remarriage, death, disability, poverty, abuse, childlessness, sexual-identity struggles, addiction, mental illness, and every other form of brokenness that comes with being human. It factors in utter failure and the opportunity to start over, because motherhood is a design that is supposed to reflect God's heart for us. This experience is not restricted to married moms with a perfect family life! God does not withdraw from brokenness. He does the opposite: He comes the closest to the brokenhearted. So does a (super)Natural Mom.

Let's look at God as the perfect Mother. This is not blasphemous. He compares Himself to a hen and a mother eagle (Matt. 23:37; Ruth 2:12; Deut. 32:11; Ps. 91:4) and talks about nursing us at His breast and comforting us as a mother does her child (Num. 11:12; Ps. 131:2; Isa. 49:15; 66:13). He even calls Himself "a woman who's having a baby" (Isa. 42:14). According to several Bible scholars, His name *El Shaddai* means "the many breasted One."[1] He knows what it's like to mother unwilling children who bite back when you invite them to be nursed. Does He resign as "mother" when His children do this? Hardly! The children of these passages are mostly thankless, unfaithful rebels. Even so, God's motherly love embraces them in all phases of their walks with Him and toward a variety of outcomes. Some respond, repent, and become His friends. Some harden their hearts and reject Him. Is it because His love lacks something, or is it perhaps because His children do?

If God, the perfect parent, has a disappointing result in many of His children, why do we assume that our families' disappointments must necessarily point to a deficiency in ourselves?

Giving In to Grace

The Old Testament ends with Malachi's powerful message from God, which I want to paraphrase, adding what I believe to be behind the significance of these words. God said them and then remained quiet for hundreds of years. Such a dramatic pause must urge us to reflect and ask one another, "What was that last thing He said? It must have been important. Wasn't it something about parenting?"

> Don't miss this: I'm sending a messenger to pave the way for how the kingdom should really work. He will come to give you a solution that will play a key part in the outcome of My day of reckoning. This is what will happen if you understand His message: the generations that have been standing with their backs to one another, disconnected and bitter, will be softened up and reconciled. They will turn around and look each other in the face with newfound love and respect. The parents will deem their children a priority, and the children will open teachable hearts toward their parents. Over this bridge from heart to heart, a rich legacy of love for God will be passed from generation to generation. This will be called "blessing," and it will cover your land if you pursue it. Godliness has been dropped like a poorly passed-on baton since the days of the kings of Israel. Read their stories again. If parents and children cannot turn their hearts toward one another, the spiritual legacy is lost too. Every generation tries to dust it off, but much is lost. This is called "the curse," and the proof of it is everywhere in your land. I want to lift this curse, and parenting is key.[2]

Evangelical believers are taught that Christ is enough and that grace will complete the work God has begun in us. In parenting, some authorities seem to add a big *but* to the burden-lifting message of mercy. When we read and listen, we get the message that we can fail elsewhere but not here. We can be forgiven everything except the wrongs we have done to our children. This idea has another devastating outcome: we are told to forgive anyone who hurts us, but there is a cultural tolerance for harboring bitterness toward our parents. It is as though they owed us perfection and we are entitled to resent them for their failures—forever. Is it any wonder that generations are pulled apart by these unrealistic expectations?

It is all about grace. Grace enables us to bend down, pick up the batons—whether we dropped them or our mothers did—and admit the failures that were ours, forgive the ones that weren't, and look toward the generation that we have written off. We reconnect by grace. Our mothering mistakes still bear down on us. They help us crack. Even that is grace. When we crack in the right way, we fall on grace and become channels of it to our children, our spouses, and other mothers. And the curse will be lifted, not by our striving to be faultless mothers, but by the life God will send through our softened hearts.

Grace saves the (un)Natural Mom and child alike. When we are in Christ, we are forgiven the worst. We are also protected from the eternal destruction sin brings. Salvation has two sides here: God will not destroy us for our sins, and He will not let the sins of others destroy us forever either. He has not given us the power to wreck our children's lives forever. We might make their lives hard, but their futures are safeguarded by a God who regards them as too valuable to be delivered into slippery hands. I believe this based on the promise in Isaiah 54:11–17. Consider the context of this passage: the older generation was taken into exile as punishment for their rebellion. One would expect this disastrous failure to destroy the chances of a good future for their children. Instead, God gave a promise to restore and redeem both generations:

> Afflicted city, storm-battered, unpitied:
>> I'm about to rebuild you with stones of turquoise,
> Lay your foundations with sapphires,
>> construct your towers with rubies,
> Your gates with jewels,
>> and all your walls with precious stones.
> All your children will have GOD for their teacher—
>> what a mentor for your children!
> You'll be built solid, grounded in righteousness,
>> far from any trouble—nothing to fear!
>> far from terror—it won't even come close!
> If anyone attacks you,
>> don't for a moment suppose that I sent them,
> And if any should attack,
>> nothing will come of it.
> I create the blacksmith
>> who fires up his forge
>> and makes a weapon designed to kill.
> I also create the destroyer—
>> but no weapon that can hurt you has ever been
>>> forged.
> Any accuser who takes you to court
>> will be dismissed as a liar.
> This is what GOD's servants can expect.
>> I'll see to it that everything works out for the best.

What a relief this truth brings! Likewise, no matter who raised you and how badly they may have done it, God's Fatherhood is what determines your destiny. For every hurt there is healing, and your key is the same as for all children who feel that their life purposes were hijacked by the failures of their parents: soften your heart, pick up the baton from the dirt, and run better than your parents did, by grace. For they too were perfect for you, not because they were anywhere close to faultless but because they started you on the journey God wrote for your life.

Tonight, whether we are living on Box-Rose Hill, serving organic food to clean kids, or in Pine-Palm Woods, just too close to the fast-food restaurant to resist going there in our pajamas after skipping bath time, by grace it is our particular kind of unnatural that makes us the perfect moms for our kids. Our sharp edges will sanctify their round bulges, and they will do the same for us. Our journeys will instruct one another because God is intentional in how He puts families together. Without that graceful knowing, we would never have stumbled into this spacious neck of the woods where every type of (un)Natural Mom and child are equally welcome.

For Reflection

1. How does the truth that God first called you Mom affect the way you think about motherhood as a godly calling? What is He trying to tell you today?

2. How would you describe the difference between a (super)Natural Mom and a supermom?

3. What are the cracks in your life that God can use to transform you if you let Him? How are you trying to hold those cracks together? What will happen if you let go?

4. Do you have a testimony of a parenting challenge that you or a fellow mom was able to take on successfully thanks to having a particular temperament?

5. Do you trust God with the ultimate welfare of your children? What stands in your way? How can you practice surrendering to Him?

Acknowledgments

To the best (un)Natural Mom I know: Mom, your thoughtful attention to details and your commitment to meet my needs modeled
the truth that I have a God who sees me and that I am worthy to be
loved. It gave me an "unfair advantage"—for life! You didn't teach
me much about cooking or sewing or gardening or knitting (I treasure that crochet lesson you gave me last Christmas, though). What
you did teach me was how to break before God on those days when
motherhood is too hard and to let Him pick me up, how to always
write thank-you notes, and how to let every child God gives me be
their own person. You gave me your writer's genes. I'm so grateful
you passed them on along with strong teeth. I've needed both on
this journey.

To my companion for life: Thank you, Louis. You sang your way
into my heart twenty-five years ago and then sang our way into the
many countries where we've ministered and learned what we now
pass on to others. You kept believing when this dream seemed out
of reach.

To my children, Idalise, Pero, and Simoné, who keep making me
more natural every day: You may deserve better, but God decided that
together we are enough. I look forward to seeing your journeys unfold
more and more and to see where He uses me in them. I am content.

Thank you to:

- everyone in my church community at KerkSonderMure (ChurchWithoutWalls) who keeps me real and grounded in God's Plan A for the world.
- all the fellow dreamers at Evergreen Parenting and Tall Trees Profiles who do battle for relationships and families with spears in one hand and building tools in the other.
- all the spiritual mothers, mentors, and fellow moms who gave input into my heart, home, and this book: Nerina, Sheila, Sonia, Zelda, Annatjie, Nantie, Margaretha, Elna, Vilna, Alet, Ria, Naudine, Paula, Jean, Marelize, Adele, Suria, Annari, Heidi, Denise, Cheryl, Lynette, Jacomine, Rika, Nanette, Hayley, Karen, Estie, and many more. This season of my life makes sense because of you.
- the team at David C Cook for taking a great risk with a writer from South Africa. I had no right to hope for a door as valued as yours to open. You have been a delight to work with every step of the way. Kyle, Verne, Erin, Jack, Cara, Nick, Susan, Tiffany, Tim, Darren, Chriscynethia, Lisa, Annette, Amy—every person who invested time, passion, and talent into making this project a reality.
- Cris Doornbos for believing in this shared calling. May God continue to use you and the entire Cook family to bless His bride all over the world.

- Kay and Julie Hirmanine who facilitated the divine appointment where this miracle started. You are true friends and servants of God.

All glory goes to the one God who did it all. Jesus, I have nothing to give unless You give it. Help me pass on all that is life giving. Thank You for the joy of being a custodian of Your evergreen hope for every (un)Natural Mom and every family.

Hettie

Notes

Chapter 2: The Counterfeit Call to Be "Natural"

1. Theodore Roosevelt, quoted in William Jennings Bryan, ed., *The World's Famous Orations, Volume 10, America: III (1861–1905)* (New York: Funk and Wagnalls, 1906).

Chapter 3: Your Own Kind of Natural

1. Ram Dass, "Ram Dass on Self Judgment," January 25, 2012, www.ramdass.org /ram-dass-on-self-judgement.

2. My adaptation of George Orwell, *Animal Farm: A Fairy Story* (London: Secker and Warburg, 1945).

Chapter 4: The (un)Natural Mom on Boxwood Boulevard

1. Connie Schultz, quoted in Vi-An Nguyen, "100 Inspiring Quotes about Moms for 100 Years of Mother's Day," *Parade*, May 9, 2014, http://parade.com /288611/viannguyen/100-inspiring-quotes-about-moms-for-100-years -of-mothers-day/.

Chapter 6: The (un)Natural Mom in the Rose Bush Garden

1. Eleanor Roosevelt, BrainyQuote, accessed March 18, 2016, www.brainyquote .com/quotes/quotes/e/eleanorroo399367.html.

2. Hillary Clinton, quoted in Robert D. McFadden, "Dorothy Rodham, Mother and Mentor of Hillary Clinton, Is Dead at 92," *New York Times*, November 1, 2011, www.nytimes.com/2011/11/02/us/dorothy-rodham-mother-of-hillary-clinton-dies-at-92.html.

Chapter 7: The (un)Natural Mom of Pine Tree Place

1. Mayim Bialik, quote in Vi-An Nguyen, "Mayim Bialik on Dealing with Divorce and Hopes for Amy and Sheldon on *The Big Bang Theory*," *Parade*, June 6, 2013, http://parade.com/20215/viannguyen/mayim-bialik-on-dealing-with-divorce-and-hopes-for-amy-and-sheldon-on-the-big-bang-theory/.

Chapter 9: The Call to (super)Natural Motherhood

1. Nathan Stone, *Names of God* (Chicago: Moody, 1944), 34.

2. Author's paraphrase of Malachi 3–4.

About the Author

Hettie grew up in Pretoria, South Africa, as the only girl among three brothers. She graduated from Menlopark High School in 1990 and studied speech pathology and audiology at the University of Pretoria. In 1992 she married Louis, then a law student. After some years of practicing respectively as a speech therapist and candidate attorney and completing two years of part-time Bible school, Louis felt called to become a performing artist and worship leader in full-time music ministry. Hettie then founded an educational upliftment project in a poor part of their city, which opened the door into full-time family ministry.

With their three small children in tow, the family traveled with Louis's band and were able to experience many cultures, giving them their first exposure to homeschooling families (then largely taboo in South Africa). They were attracted to what seemed to be the best solution for their family and their children's emerging learning styles. Hettie also became fascinated by the various approaches to parenting they encountered around the world. It enlarged her perspective and became the foundation for three parenting books. The first, *Growing Kids with Character*, released in 2007 and became a bestseller, now in its tenth printing in Afrikaans and fourth in English. It deals with temperament profiles or "tree types," which help parents determine their temperament, and how to discipline, encourage, prune, and grow each individual child. The second book, *Growing Kids through Healthy Authority*, focuses on parenting-style preferences and helps parents embrace their differences and use them to their children's advantage.

In 2008 she was accredited by OTI Consulting (Singapore) to present DiSC profile workshops, team building seminars, and training in team dimensions and time mastery. Hettie then developed the Evergreen Parenting Course and in 2009 started training facilitators to present the course in South Africa and around the world. The training team has grown, and there are now facilitators in Namibia, Botswana, Egypt, Macedonia, the United Arab Emirates, Australia, and New Zealand. Courses for the training of preschool teachers, elementary school teachers, caregivers at orphanages and illiterate parents have flowed from the Evergreen Parenting Course.

Along with Annatjie van Zyl, Hettie developed Tall Trees Profiles, personality- and leadership-style profiles. Their training division has equipped more than two hundred facilitators to use these profiles in schools, companies, churches, and families with the aim to facilitate personal and career growth and to strengthen relationships through a better understanding of individuals and their interaction with others.

Hettie's third book, *Cultivating Compassionate Discipline*, was published in 2012 and deals with discipline at home and in schools. Hettie wrote the book with the aim of bringing parents and teachers together in the fight against the decline of healthy discipline in South Africa's schools. A computer program, the Compassionate Discipline School System, is based on this book and is an online tool that extends parenting principles into schools and makes classroom discipline easier and more consistent (www.cdschool.co.za). It has been approved by South Africa's minister of basic education and is also part of a school intervention program developed in cooperation with UNISA, called Pele².

Hettie has joined Focus on the Family Africa for an annual talk tour since 2013. On these tours she speaks to parents and teachers about parenting, temperament, and discipline, and she also ministers to women about forgiveness, overcoming fear and embracing true freedom. Hettie regularly writes for Christian and secular women's magazines and has produced nearly four hundred parenting inserts for national television in South Africa.

She is involved in raising funds and awareness against human trafficking with Operation Mobilization's Freedom Climb (now called the Freedom Challenge). She joined their first climb of Kilimanjaro in 2012 and the Alps in 2015 and coauthored their Bible study guide, *Knowing God and Doing Justice*.

Hettie is an avid deer hunter and scrapbooker who also enjoys open-water swimming, having participated in several one- and two-mile races. She is a self-confessed coffee snob who imports her own instant Starbucks to South Africa so that she can drink "decent coffee" on her adventures and speaking tours. She has many more mountain peaks on her bucket list and does not easily pass up on adventure.

She also works as an adviser and fund gatekeeper for South Africa's Business for Empowerment Trust (B4ET), which channels Black Economic Empowerment funds toward worthy causes, including the Mohau Child Care Centre and Thuthuzela Home (for children orphaned, affected, and infected by HIV/AIDS) and End

It SA (an initiative with a rescue program and safehouse for human-trafficking and sex-slavery victims).

Between homeschooling her three kids and joining her husband on his ministry outreaches, Hettie has presented talks and courses in South Africa, Ukraine, Australia, New Zealand, England, the United States, Namibia, Mozambique, Botswana, and the United Arab Emirates. Her key convictions are that there is hope for every individual and any relationship and that there is no place or circumstance so dark that God can't turn it around for good.

Hettie, Louis, and their three children make their home in Pretoria, South Africa.